Dedication:

*To Ma and Pa Johnson, Cora's folks,
for teaching me about country life.*

WEST OF WITTY

Minne-Sconsin Stories and Femails

Rick A. Wehler

Henschel
HAUS
Milwaukee, Wisconsin

Published by
HenschelHAUS Publishing, Inc.
www.henschelHAUSbooks.com

ISBN: 978-159598-800-3
E-ISBN: 978159598-801-0
Library of Congress Control Number (LCCN): 2020951695

Cover photo: Brothers Toby and Jerry Wehler standing in the ancient Claw Tree at Westwoods.

Praise for *West of Witty* and author Rick Wehler:

I have had the extreme pleasure of reading several of Rick Wehler's books, including a few snippets from this one prior to its publication. Rick has a knack for telling a story that has caused me to smile often, chuckle frequently, and actually laugh out loud on many occasions. I have yet to figure out how he can take ordinary events in life and turn them into humor, but he's a master of that art. Occasionally he has a very poignant story to tell, and that one gets every bit of his emotion. He's an everyday guy who wants to share his life with the rest of us, and we are all the richer for the experience.
—*Patricia Hedetniemi, retired nurse and an avid reader.*

Rick is spot on with his stories. They are funny, yet so relatable. I have shared his books with my whole family who have also laughed along. This series is very hard to put down once you start it. I haven't known Rick very long, but by reading his books, I feel like I've grown up with his family. I can't wait for the next book.
—*Lisa Brand: Grandma, retired, and the wife of a Vegman.*

You're sure to enjoy this delightful, witty book. You'll laugh as each hilarious story unfolds and teaches us that there is humor in every corner of daily life. Rick's clever use of wordsmithing puts a "play" on words like no other author. His life-long love affair with his wife, the "Dish" is always at the forefront of his escapades. Rick has a real knack for storytelling and after you read this book, you're going to want to buy the other three in the set. That is if you don't already own them. Enjoy!
—*Diane Ricker, retired IT professional.*

Rick's books, West of Witty, North of Normal, South of Superior, and East of Excelsior, encompass (see what I did there) his funny life experiences. The books will allow you to discover that life doesn't have to be "normal." He takes everyday experiences and adds his interpretation of what is, or in his case, what isn't normal! Do you want to have an entire Scandinavian town upset with you? Then win most of the turkeys at Turkey Bingo and see what happens.
—*Mike Erickson, also from Excelsior, a classmate of Rick's from the last century and millennium. He went East. I went West.*

Having thoroughly enjoyed Rick's first three books, I eagerly await his fourth. Rick's writing is full of light-hearted humor and wit, and can be read and reread with the same enjoyment.
—*Joe Campolo Jr. Author, The Kansas NCO trilogy.*

Other books by Rick Wehler:

North of Normal: Minne-Sconsin Stories

South of Superior: More Minne-Sconsin Stories

East of Excelsior: A Senior's Minne-Sconsin Stories

TABLE OF CONTENTS

BOOK II—FEMAILS

PREFACE

This, the fourth book in the Minne-Sconsin series, has two main sections: stories and femails; and as added attractions: afterthoughts, quips, quotes and banter battles.

Minne-Sconsin Stories are tales of the lighter side of life's happenings, and memories that were still available to me at the time. I follow a few of the stories with "Afterthoughts," those ideas that show up after I've finished writing a story and I grumble, "I'm not going to rewrite it."

Femails are a collection of laughable emails exchanged with my baby sisters Rhonda, aka Ru, and Sandi, aka Bun. They date back to 1998 when Ru first urged me to save them. I've selected a few from the compilation, edited them so as to be a little less inappropriate, and shared them in date order as we wrote them.

I mentioned to my wife Cora, "I was a tad screwy 22 years ago."

She replied, "Nothing has changed but your age...and the tad."

Oftentimes, I'll write a quip or a quote, or engage in a banter battle with Cora, which I lose nine times out of ten because I only battle nine times. I've selected several from the compilations, edited them so as to be a little less inappropriate, and shared them between the stories.

My wife's senior-citizen aunt said, "Rick, these afterthoughts, quips, quotes and banter battles interrupt my thought train. They must do that to you too."

Cora commented, "Rick doesn't have many cars in his thought train. It doesn't even have a caboose."

Considering such constructive criticism, and not wishing to stuff the afterthoughts, quips, quotes and banter battles into my missing caboose as the ladies suggested, I considered skipping them altogether. I swore to myself, "F-forget skipping them, and

i

forget a little less inappropriate! If they make me laugh, then I'm stuffing them, as is, into...the book."

—Rick Wehler

AFTERTHOUGHTS

I mentioned to the ladies, "I didn't plan on adding a fourth book to the Minne-Sconsin Stories trilogy. It just happened."

Auntie advised, "More people would read your "trilogy" if you'd do book signings, videos, podcasts, and speaking engagements."

Cora replied, "Rick doesn't care to be heavily medicated."

###

Brussels Sprouts and Dog Food

Preface

I n this story, I'm sharing two early chapters of my novel relationship with Cora's family: her parents Ma and Pa Johnson, brothers Richie and Glen, and their mongrel farm dog Penny. (Cora's sister Bev was married and no longer living at home.) Ma, Pa and Penny are gone, but they live on in my memories of our times together.

Our first trip as an engaged couple to visit Cora's family at their 1890s farmhouse in Henning, Minnesota, population 800 on a good day, happened late on October 30th, 1970. I parked our car in the driveway; and we waded through snow drifts, entered their side-porch, knocked, opened the kitchen door, and stepped onto a rippled, slanted, linoleum floor. I spotted old, creaky cupboards and a 1950s Formica table with matching chairs. I thought, "Man, this place is cool."

Cora's five-foot-eight, well-muscled, nine-year-old, little brother Glen stood just inside the door. He looked at me with a questioning gaze as I took off my stocking cap, keyed in on my long hair and mocked, "Hippy, hippy, hippy."

I looked back at him and threatened, "If you say that again, I'll dump you in a snowdrift."

He replied in a sing-songy voice, "Hippy, hippy, hippy." I picked him up, walked outside, and dropped him into a snowdrift. I returned and introduced myself to Ma, Pa and Richie who were seated at the kitchen table. Ma took it in stride. Pa and Richie were cautiously amused.

Bedtime was close at hand so we didn't spend much time visiting. I planned on collecting a goodnight kiss from Cora, but Ma wouldn't let me anywhere near her.

Cora slept on the main-level, living-room couch by the floor furnace while I slept in a bed upstairs where the only available heat floated up from downstairs through a ceiling grate. I made myself as comfortable as possible on a thin mattress laid out on a wire-mesh support. I covered up with two quilts, wore all of my clothes, and my coat, stocking cap, gloves and boots. I took note of the frost-covered windows, watched my breath drift in the room, and imagined Ma laughing at that pansy, city boy.

The next day, Halloween, Ma costumed Glen as a girl. I objected strenuously. She didn't tell me to shut the hell up, but I could see it in her glare, a trait that Cora inherited.

II

I graduated from college May 6th of 1971, and accepted a full-time job as a produce clerk at a big grocery store in Brooklyn Park, Minnesota.

On that day, Cora leveled Ma's glare and claimed, "You said that we'd get married at the Lutheran church in Henning after you graduated."

I replied, "You're right. How about six months from today?"

Cora said, "November 6th. That works. I'll let Ma know."

I worked a crazy amount of hours, daytime in the produce department and overnight in the grocery department stocking shelves. Along the way, I made some friends who were willing to help me out with an idea.

While stocking shelves, we turned up unsaleable cans, dented or without labels, and put them into empty apple boxes that I'd saved from working in produce. We emptied torn bags of flour and sugar into five-gallon buckets that the bakery folks had given me. I stacked the boxes and buckets in an out-of-the-way, backroom hallway.

Not long after we got married, the collection of damaged groceries looked as if it would max out the hauling capacity of our 1968, Ford Torino sedan. I approached the assistant store manager and haggled over a price. We agreed upon two dollars per box or bucket. After I showed him the receipt, Cora and I crammed every available space in the Torino.

Before we left, I checked with the produce manager to see if he had any damaged fruits or vegetables that I could buy. I purchased several over-wrapped trays of Brussels sprouts with some yellowed leaves for a quarter per package. We found room for them somewhere, and took off on the three-hour drive north to the Johnson home.

Pa and Richie worked for a traveling construction company that did business in the warm months of the year. During the winter, they were both laid off. Ma worked part-time at a local bar, Boo and Ruby's, pouring fifty-cent beers and frying burgers. The winter months were lean.

We arrived at Ma and Pa's place Friday evening and sat around at the kitchen table. I listened to stories about recent Henning happenings: who died, who didn't, who moved from one place to another, who's romancing whom, and more.

Ma and Cora were the talkers. Pa and Richie, per normal, sat impassively, and I enjoyed the ambiance. When the conversation centered on town, about five miles distant, Pa pointed his right thumb back over his shoulder and spoke when the women acknowledged his gesture.

After a fun visit, Cora told the family about the groceries in the car. Ma watched as the rest of us unloaded the boxes and buckets, and set them on the kitchen floor.

We sat at the table while Ma pulled the lid off of the first apple box. I've seldom seen anyone as excited as she, like a five-year-old opening a gift from Santa on Christmas morning.

Ma opened the rest of the boxes, with Glen's help, and began sorting the cans into categories, and planning future meals. Ma held unlabeled cans close to her ear, gave them a shake, made her best guess as to the contents, and added them to the proper stacks. Glen loaded the goodies not needed for the next couple of weeks back into the boxes for Richie to move to the root cellar.

Finally, Ma opened the box of Brussels sprouts, She took out the packages and set them on the table. Pa's face lit up. He opened one of them, grabbed a Brussels sprout and peeled off the yellowed leaves. Pa looked over his shoulder at me, smiled broadly, even his eyes smiled, displayed the Brussels sprout, and took a careful bite with his remaining teeth. I could hear the crunch. He looked back at me again and smiled as he finished the first sprout and went after another one.

Ma kept sorting cans, and Pa kept smiling and crunching Brussels sprouts while I sat back enraptured by the scene.

The root cellar was a big hole in the ground beneath the side-porch. Richie opened the trap door, climbed down the dirt-covered, rickety stairs, flipped on the dangling lightbulb, and positioned the cans on shelves mounted into the earthen walls that already held Ma's homemade, canned goods. He set the extra buckets of flour and sugar on the floor next to wash tubs that were filled with apples from their ancient trees, squash from Ma's gardens, and potatoes gleaned from farmers' fields, all buried and preserved in sand.

Saturday evening, as we sat at the kitchen table, Ma latched onto her hand-held can opener and began cranking open the cans that she had set aside for dinner, three each of small, whole potatoes, green beans, and unlabeled, best-guess, corned-beef hash. She emptied the potatoes and beans into their own pots on the gas stove. Meanwhile, Pa was happily munching on Brussels sprouts. Ma opened the first unlabeled can, sniffed it, and unfazed, dumped the dog food into Penny's bowl.

# # # # #

THE COST OF LIVING

Two months before my heart surgery, I set a plan: lay low for two weeks before the procedure and four weeks thereafter. Within that time frame, I read a dozen unintellectual books, and wrote several stories along the same lines, which I saved on Google Docs. Once I could find some humor in it, I even wrote a story about my heart surgery. Hopefully, these healthful activities will strengthen my mind and heart before the surgery bills arrive.

I've discovered that my eyesight has crossed the tripping point, much to the delight of common household hazards. Reading books and reviewing my writing has become a challenge. I've learned to borrow large-print books from the library, and increase the Google Docs script to 200%.

With Wifey's encouragement, I scheduled an eye checkup at a highly recommended venue located in a repurposed church building, Cross Eye Clinic.

I confessed to Dr. Deacon, "My eyes are on the path to destruction."

He comforted, "We'll do an exam, the unabridged version, and we'll take pictures of the dark side of your eyes."

Dr. Deacon guided me into a private room and said, "Be calm, my son. Set your chin on this lower support, lean your forehead against the upper support, and look through the phoropter lenses at the screen." He performed the unabridged tests, and took flash photographs of the insides of my wide-open eyes.

Based on my interpretation of his lengthy sermon, my eyesight had gone to hell. To my further dismay, he insisted on downloading and sharing the photos with me. Dr. Deacon exclaimed, "Holy sh#&! Take a look at these photographs. Your vision can be saved. Unfortunately, our creator won't be able to produce lenses of that strength. Here's your lens prescription and our Cross Eye

Clinic calling card. Feel free to contact us if we can be of service." He added, "Please pay the usher at the front desk on your way out."

Thanks to Cora's smartphone, we discovered a clinic close by that specializes in powerful lenses, Bugg Ide Clinic. The congenial Mr. Ide guided us through a myriad of lenses with special properties and prices. He recommended, "These thin, polymer, Teflon-coated, glare-inhibiting, progressive lenses are just right for you."

I asked, "How much?"

He answered, "$190...each."

Being the pleasant person that I am not when it comes to the cost of living, I proclaimed, "I'll take two!"

Cora and I selected a set of frames priced at $68. I mentioned to her, "Bugg Ide Clinic doesn't offer monocle frames for $34."

I viewed the final bill, $448, and blurted, "Outstanding! No sales tax."

Mr. Ide boasted, "Both lenses have a two-year replacement warranty that covers scratches." He didn't seem concerned, having estimated my smart-ass life expectancy.

I replied, "Bugger, a shame that warranty wasn't available when I was growing up in Blackeye, Minnesota."

Ide added, "Due to the complexity of the project, your new glasses won't be ready for at least ten business days."

I commented, "Business days...that discounts the weekends and February's holidays, including Groundhog's Day, Valentine's Day, Presidents Day and the leap-year. Will my new specs be available by the Ides of March?"

He said curtly, "We'll call when your glasses arrive. Here's our Bugg Ide Clinic calling card. Feel free to contact us if we can be of any further help. Please pay my pupil at the front desk on your way out."

Along with heart surgery, eyeglasses are just another factor in the cost of living.

March 25th, the dentist...

#####

AFTERTHOUGHTS

When considering buying new glasses, I commented, "Cora, I've cleaned my glasses three times. The newspaper is still blurry. It must be screwed up."

Cora replied, "It's your eyes that are screwed up."

I shot back, "You still look nineteen to me."

She countered, "See what I mean?"

###

I picked up my new, high-tech glasses, looked at myself in the mirror and said, "That can't be right."

Cora comforted, "You'll adjust. I have. Could take a while."

###

THIS MORNING

This morning, while at the table, contemplating my choices in life; I've concluded that breakfast is my third favorite meal of the day.

Arising from a warm bed and a hot wife to breakfast is not much to my liking. I lay my clothes out the night before, which has nearly eliminated comatose mismatches, but not my feeble fashion sense. Doing so doesn't overcome my balance issues while removing layers of jammies and shoving my size-13 feet through size-11 jean legs.

Cora bought me a new set of hard-soled slippers, not long ago. They remain stiff and unappreciative of my socks, which match this morning. It's difficult not to be awakened by slippers slapping the kitchen tile.

On occasion, just before bed, I'd make an offhand guess as to which breakfast choices would displease me the least and set them on the counter, with the exception of toast. I discontinued the practice as invariably the next morning, I'd reassess my half-assed selections.

This morning, with jeans in place, naked feet and a bare counter, I unclosed the breakfast-food cabinet in hopes of finding an acceptable meal. Unfortunately, I'd previously opened the family-sized boxes of cereal, removed the cellophane bags, placed the empty boxes into the recycle bin, and spilled each cereal into its own XL, snap-on-covered, foggy, plastic canister. I say foggy with the kindest regards as they in no way measure up to my early morning vision.

As best I can remember, the canisters contain Frosted Flakes, Wheat Chex, Raisin Bran, Grape Nuts, Honey-Nut Cheerios, Rice Chex, Corn Pops and Cap'n Crunch; all of which are indistinguishable between 5:30 a.m. and 7 a.m. Thanks to probiotics, I'm able to drown the crunchy, sugary cereals in regular milk, lactose intact, enhancing the sweetness of the bottom-of-the-bowl residue.

Available in the original boxes are Coco Wheats and Quaker Oats, but I reserve those hot cereals for the frigid winter mornings when I've screwed up the overnight thermostat setting, and I'm not afraid of the stove.

This morning, I set every foggy container on the counter because I don't have to go any freaking where. I can take my time to uncover their identities and make an unconscious choice.

Frosted Flakes is my favorite breakfast cereal. This morning, I'm feeling a bit put off, remembering Tony the Tiger's toothless smile, a victim of his own concoction.

Wheat Chex, Raisin Bran, Grape Nuts and Honey-Nut Cheerios are tasty, whole-grain, depressingly-brown cereals, which challenge my probiotics, my wish not to need whole grains, and my hopes for a cheerful morning. I'm beginning to question my choices in life.

Rice Chex is great! Their light-tan color is a lift, but if I don't indulge quickly after their baptism, the Chex and the tablespoon of sugar melt into one distasteful puddle of sludge.

Corn Pops are a cheery bright yellow and they don't require milk to be soggy.

Cap'n Crunch makes no apologies for its mind-boggling, sugar content. At one time, I thought that Cap'n Crunch Crunch Berries would be a healthier choice but dismissed the idea. I couldn't resist referring to it as Cap'n Crunch Dingle Berries, the cereal killer.

This morning, breakfast is toast.

#####

QUIPS AND QUOTES: COVID-19

I mentioned to Cora, "The federal bailout offers $1,200 per adult and $500 per child."

She replied, "We'll receive $1,700: $1,200 for me and $500 for you."

While walking, I spotted a lady pushing a baby buggy heading towards me on the sidewalk. She passed within my six-foot, social-distancing boundary. No problem. I'm sure her perfume killed off any Covid-19 floaters.

I'm tired of social distancing. Cora should invite me over for a play date.

Cora, you jigsaw puzzle people need medication.

I filled up on gas for 99 cents per gallon and a Culver's milkshake for $3.89 per quart.

During the stay-at-home order, the local cable service is offering a couple weeks of free movie channels. I surfed the selection and found a late-night movie entitled, "Scared Topless." No thanks. Not the right time for horror movies.

###

"Forget this covid crisis. I need to get outside. It's our first warm spring day. I'm going to wear shorts and a tank shirt, and cut the grass."

"Hubber, the neighbors will be gone soon. Why don't you spare them and wait for a bit."

"Wifey, sure, then it'll be warmer and I can go barefoot too."

"Hubber, covid crisis or not. I'm leaving the area."

To get some outside time, I asked Cora to go for a walk with me. I wasn't planning on a 5k.

A first: my dentist cancelled my appointment before I did.

Covid information is like toilet paper. When you need it, it's better to have too much than not enough.

While on a social-distancing walk, I asked Cora, "Who was that masked man?"

She replied, "The Lone Stranger."

The Covid nasal test is like a prostate exam with a long-handled toothbrush.

The world is ending. No frickin' garage sales. I need underwear!

Stay-at-home, meh. My calendar is as crammed with the lack of social activities as it always has been.

###

PAINTING THE DECK RAILING

We agreed that I should update the gray paint on our second-story deck railing. Cora and I have lived here for eighteen years. I've had time to consider the project.

Nine years ago, I replaced the rotting deck boards and steps, and left the gray railing untouched. At that time, Cora insisted that the new boards remain unpainted, the *au naturel* look—an interesting choice. Many times I've offered her my *au naturel* look and found it less than appreciated.

Thankfully, I won't paint myself into a corner and grant Cora the opportunity to laugh until she cries as when I painted the stairs leading to the basement by starting on the main floor. I can always jump off the deck.

To start, I removed much of the old paint with a metal scraper that I'd recently become familiar with when I asked Cora to scratch a spot on my back that I couldn't reach.

Paint the deck railing, no big deal:

- There are more 4-sided uprights than stars in the visible universe.

- Every surface is 3-coats thirsty.

The flocks of birds that feast at our feeders don't seem to understand that it's inconsiderate to cast their seed shells upon, hop around on, and whitewash wet, gray paint.

With uncharacteristic forethought, I had purchased a pair of cheap, plastic, safety glasses to wear over my new high-tech, octafocal lenses. Halfway through each day of the painting project, I remembered to remove the safety glasses from my hat brim and employ them.

I didn't bother with an apron as Cora felt that the paint dribbles would enhance my garage-sale clothing.

The further I progressed, the more items attacked my OCD:

- The fresh paint doesn't match the old paint on the support beams.

- The unpainted deck floor and steps don't look right anymore.

- The underside and the ends of every (freaking) board should be painted.

- Don't forget the insides of the knot holes.

I mumbled, "Maybe I should just stay inside and close the curtains."

The painting project took less than a week. The wildlife that visits our deck: the aforementioned birds; and squirrels, raccoons, opossums, chipmunks, and the occasional tree frog seem confused, often checking Google Maps. I trust that we will all adapt, eventually.

I commented, "This morning's rain is floating water bubbles on the deck."

Cora replied, "Sort of like you did in the bathtub last night."

#####

PARAPHRASE

Me: Doc, my chest hurts and it's not due to heart trouble!

Doc pressing on my chest, repeatedly: Does this hurt? Does this hurt? Does this hurt?

Me answering, repeatedly: Yes. Hell, yes. Damn!

Doc: Tell me about your former job, hobbies and hazardous pursuits.

Me: I managed produce departments in grocery stores, lifted crates, and filled displays. My hobbies are weight lifting and bike riding, and I married a Norwegian woman.
Since retirement, twelve years ago, I work part-time at a grocery store, continue my hobbies, and I'm still married. I've taken up writing, backpacking, camping, and forestry.

Doc: You've earned your chest pain and continue to earn it. Recovering from chest cartilage and tendon damage can take three to nine months. If you continue to lift heavy weights, you're not going to heal, and I've heard about Norwegian women.

Me: Doc, my posture sucks. I lean forward so my chest won't hurt, which makes lifting all the more difficult.

Doc *paraphrase:* Practice good posture, stop lifting heavy weights, Einstein, and take these pain pills.

Me: If I take pain pills, I won't be able to tell if a heavy lift is hurting me or not.

Doc *paraphrase:* If you keep dickin' around liftin' heavy sh*t, you're never gonna heal, dumbass!

That conversation took place in early January. Since then, I've taken a leave of absence from my part-time job, discontinued weightlifting, three or four times, and I remain married.

I haven't made any progress on the chest pain.

The pills disguise the pain when I'm required to be in the company of anyone besides the wife. She shuts down my complaints in a flash; makes my chest ache just to think about it. Drugged and floating about pain-free, I absent-mindedly smiled while helping the new neighbors unload their moving van. I experienced similar effects when I shoveled us out from a February snowstorm, and chopped the ice loose from our sidewalk, driveway, second-story deck and roof while in my pajamas. As it's mid-March at this writing, the upcoming forestry season weighs heavily upon me. I must transplant dozens of white pine saplings, and prune a host of their 80-foot-tall parents with my mega-manly, Crapsman pole-chainsaw. I have to stack the shorn branches into massive heaps; otherwise they'll faceplant me as I backpack through the forest.

I plan to skip the three- and six-month follow-up appointments with Doc because I won't have to paraphrase his comments.

#####

NAMA WAS NOT PLEASED

Our son Andy called Cora early in the evening to report that his wifey, Kristin, is having labor pains, and they're heading to the hospital. So Nama Cora invited the grandsons, 10-year-old Grasyn and 4-year-old Lucas, to stay with us overnight.

After dinner, we boys ate stuff we weren't supposed to eat: Brach's candy corn, Kemps, peppermint, bon-bon ice cream, Oreos, Lay's potato chips, and homemade sugar cookies, downing all with chocolate milk.

Nama was not pleased.

We played chase games, raced sandbox dump trucks across the living room carpet, tuned the radio to hard-rock music, loud, battled with garage-sale boxing gloves, and invented superhero names such as Firefly, Squitoman, and Boogerboy. And we stayed up way past my bedtime.

Nama was not pleased.

Nama convened a late-night, family meeting to discuss sleeping arrangements, and impose a bedtime. I had planned a "camp-out" on our upstairs loft, utilizing a tent, sleeping bags, air mattresses, flashlights and battery-operated lanterns, treat bags, rude noises, and scary stories.

No, she wasn't.

My double-crossing grandsons had their own plans. Grasyn claimed the queen-size bed in the guestroom, all to himself. Lucas favored the soft carpeting on the guestroom floor, his selection of blankets, and the personal pillow that he'd brought along from home. Both chose to read books, privately, by flashlight and lantern light.

So here am I, jammies on, brushing my teeth over the bathroom sink—no tent, no sleeping bag, no air mattress, no

16

flashlight or lantern, no treat bag, plenty of rude noises, no scary stories, no grandsons, and no wife. She insisted on sleeping upstairs, without my company, to watch over the grandsons. (I'm a bad influence and, and she's no fun at all.) I'll be braving the 14-below-zero winter's night in our bed by myself.

As I stare into the mirror above the sink, reflecting on the evening, toothpaste dribbling onto my jammies, I wonder, "Why is the word 'OFFLINE' that's stenciled on my jammie shirt backwards in the mirror? Is my shirt inside out?"

My telepathic reflection answered, "Just take your weary mind and body to bed, old man, and camp out on Cora's side."

The following morning, Andy called to say that Kristin's labor pains were a false alarm; no baby yet.

Nama was not pleased.

#####

MY SIGNATURE IS NOT REQUIRED

I began writing stories about the lighter side of life's happenings around the beginning of the millennium. Demonstrating intelligence many a level above my I.Q. and a new found confidence in computers, subsequent to the Y2K debacle, I routinely activated the "save as" option.

In 2015, I perused the stockpile and wondered if I shouldn't do something with them. Then and there, I purposed to author three books and uncover a publisher. I sorted the stories into three collections based upon subject, length, and the probability that someone, anyone, would understand and appreciate the humor.

As it turned out, HenschelHaus published one book per year starting in 2016. In 2019, with the goal accomplished, I decided to make an effort to sell some.

Jim, the manager at our local Hy-Vee grocery store, offered to purchase ten of each book, host a book signing, and have his assistant manager, Jake, handle the details. Jake and I agreed upon 11a.m. Saturday of Easter weekend for the event.

My quick-witted wife, often quoted in my writing, Cora the Dish, agreed to attend the function. She's an outgoing, down-to-earth woman everyone loves. In that fashion, she'll visit and laugh with customers, and highlight my skills. All I have to do is shield myself from her wit and sign books.

Jake set us up with a table just inside the entry doors by the shopping carts. It was breezy and a bit chilly. We felt much like Walmart greeters as we smiled, nodded, and well-wished those customers who didn't avoid eye contact.

On occasion, a customer stopped by, visited with Cora, and admired her husband-bashing humor.

Cora, with a thumb pointing over her shoulder, said to Clara, a senior-citizen lady, "He wrote these books. The partial titles,

North of Normal, South of Superior, and *East of Excelsior* describe his sense of humor."

Clara smiled and asked, "East of Excelsior?"

Cora explained, "East of Excelsior is where he grew up, but besides the town, Excelsior can also mean 'the utmost' or in his case, 'shredded paper.'"

Clara giggled and said, "I'm going to buy *East of Excelsior.* I'm visiting from North Carolina, and I want to take something home that is truly Midwestern."

Cora, once again with a thumb pointing over her shoulder, joked, "Take him, no charge, but no return!"

I thought, "If Cora makes such an offer to a lady forty years younger than Clara, I'll consider the move."

Clara broke out laughing and said, "He'd like North Carolina. Cora, would you please sign my book?"

Cora replied, "Sure, would you like Rick's autograph too? Don't worry. No one will be able to read it."

Another lady, Harriette, while conversing with Cora said, "My husband is beginning to suffer memory problems. He'll like this book, *North of Normal.*"

Cora smiled and said, "Thanks. I hope you and your husband will laugh together."

Harriette requested, "Cora, would you sign our book please?"

Cora answered, "I'd love too. Would you like Rick's signature as well?"

She replied, "You can sign his name, underneath yours."

After Harriette departed, Cora whispered, "She and I have something in common."

Unfortunately, I asked, "Oh, yeah? How so?"

Cora replied, "We both have husbands who seem a bit off the mark."

I shot back, "That's it. Sign me out."

#####

ACCOMMODATION

Somewhere along the path to the American dream, the simple life has escaped me. Several aspects of survival other folks find simplistic are complex to my understanding. Today's case-in-point is air conditioning.

According to family folklore, within my genealogy there exists a full-blooded, female, Spanish ancestor. Perhaps her gifted genes explain my inordinate heat tolerance. I enjoy temperatures ranging in the 90s with the humidity vying for digital precedence. I'm not discomposed by profuse sweating. I merely wring out my clothing, often. Friends, though, are not found in my proximity—must be the heat. My wife, the Dish, explains that most of humanity has been programmed to appreciate the 70s. I agree with her contention. That decade contained some of the happiest times of my life.

While lounging on my deck chair, my repose is challenged by a myriad of boisterous air conditioners mocking the nature of the halcyon summer day. Throughout the winter, my neighbors shun the cold temperatures by hibernating within their comfortable, climate-controlled caverns. As summer is now in control, nearby residents are again hidden within their air-conditioned retreats. The Dish is among their company.

In order to hope for overnight companionship on warm evenings, I've been compelled to enlist the assistance of whole-house air conditioning, a service which would seem much cheaper than a rented bed partner or marriage counseling. The Dish and I have reached a reasonable accommodation. We activate the winter-in-summer device at the ambient temperature of 78 degrees. With this compromise in mind, I don't understand the purpose of Dish's all-encompassing pajamas. I should be ogling her lack of apparel.

ACCOMMODATION

When our air conditioner activates, it sounds as if someone has dropped a soup spoon down the conditioner's metal shaft colliding in sequence with a descending trail of aluminum pie pans. Why should I have to wake every twelve minutes as the system reignites to curse an instrument that dreams of playing percussion in a bluegrass band?

This evening, I clandestinely altered our accommodation by changing the air conditioner's overnight setting to 65 degrees. The *restus-interruptus* device will now continue running until hell freezes over. At least I'll have relative quiet and matrimonial company.

When the Dish is away, the miserable machine slumbers. I alone thaw in the heat and sweat stain the furniture with impunity. Neighbors, who needs them? They only appear in May, weather dependent.

#####

BANTER BATTLES

Cora purchased a lottery ticket at the service desk of our local grocery store.

The attendant commented, "Good luck."

I replied, "I hope she doesn't win $400 million because she'll leave me at home and travel the world with the boy toys of her choice."

The attendant laughed and said, "So would I."

Cora added, "I'd do that if I won $10."

The attendant nearly had a stroke laughing.

I didn't.

While proofreading one of my stories Cora advised, "You need a comma here."

I looked and replied, "I don't think so."

She shot back, "A comma or a coma. Your choice."

###

I'm crawling on the kitchen floor with a spray bottle of Windex when Cora walks in.

I explain, "I'm cleaning up all of your drips."

She replied, "Spray yourself."

###

I asked, "Cora, do you want to take me out?"

She clapped her hands enthusiastically and answered, "Yessssssss!"

I added, "I meant dinner."

###

CHEERIO

Traditionally, a couple weeks before Easter, I buy one 10 oz. bag of Brach's Jelly Beans at a ridiculously expensive price, in part to remind myself of the upcoming holiday. There are seldom more than six cherry jelly beans in the entire freaking bag, but no shortage of pink, whatever flavor that is.

Today, Tuesday after Easter, is nearly the best markdown-candy holiday of the year, second only to Halloween. To date, I've eaten less than half of last Halloween's haul. Marriage has its disadvantages.

I'm standing in aisle #4, the markdown aisle, of our local grocery store. This year, management decided to forego the gradual markdowns over the next three weeks and priced it all at 50 percent off. They'll be sold out in mere days. I've got decisions to make.

The prepackaged Easter baskets are a wholesale screwing even at half price. I'm not into getting screwed, unless … never mind.

Chocolate bunnies. No, I've learned to discount such purchases. The ears are tasty but the hollow head and body disappear in two bites. It's like ordering a chocolate-dipped cone from Dairy Queen and finding no "ice cream" in the middle.

Five one-pound bags of jelly beans should net me nearly six ounces of cherry-flavored beans. Wifey will sort out the black beans for the goth, licorice-monster loan officer at our local credit union, who'll in turn grant us an extra month to pay up. I'll set aside the pink jellies for next Halloween's trick-or-treaters.

Thanks to Hershey's, I'll indulge in the heart-healthy aspects of solid, chocolate bunny eggs—three pounds.

Peeps. Well, I'm not much of a fan, but slicing up a nest of Peeps Easter bunnies, and sprinkling their remains on my Cheerios, adds color, and keeps the sugar bowl in the cupboard.

Consumption of copious quantities of sugar is detrimental to my long-term health, but a significant burst to my short-term energy level, a reasonable trade-off.

After three bowls of embellished, whole-grain Cheerios, I headed out to our 65-acre, forested property, along with my Crapsman, pole chainsaw, and enough chocolate bunny eggs to sustain my heart health and energy level. Man, I was a manic Paul Bunyan, cutting up and stacking dead trees without mercy.

Upon homecoming, I felt uncomfortable, off balance, and my chest hurt. The emergency-room doctor, Henry D. Aeth, sporting a British accent, stated, "My dear boy, your blood pressure is 149/100 and pulse rate is 132. We're going to set up an IV, administer some fluids, medications, and follow through with an MRA and a smattering of blood tests."

Two hours later, Dr. D. Aeth informed, "Your MRA and blood tests came back rather well, except for an inexplicably high level of glucose (sugar). Your BP and pulse have calmed down to 97/55 and 56 respectively. Perhaps, the problem was due to a short-term energy burst. Take this medication until you meet with your healthcare provider. Cheerio!"

#####

SWELL

F
our years and seven months ago, June 1, 2007, I retired from my middle-management position at a Midwestern, grocery store concern. At that time, I asked my Norwegian wife of 40 years, Cora the Dish, to retire along with me. She answered with conviction, "I'm not staying home with you 24/7." To this day, the Dish continues her employment while I remain here at home, her harbored, house-hunk, or as she says her humble, house husband.

I began this—my second full-time career—by expanding the part-time position I'd held for the previous 35 years and five months. Let me state for the record that I do have several hunk hobbies, for instance bicycling, weight-lifting, and forestry work. Such endeavors are necessary to maintain the trim, muscular form so appreciated by the Dish. Yeah, that's right.

This afternoon, I took a break from my chores to visit with a former coworker, a.ka. Marty Malone, via Facebook. Although we haven't seen each other since she accepted a management job with a grocery store company and moved to Arizona, our friendship remains solid.

I'll share the latter part of our correspondence, albeit, this section is a tad one-sided:

Rick: I've been looking for something less mundane to occupy myself this winter because I'm no longer attuned to the cold of outside activities. So you'd have a retirement job for me in management? I'd promise to control my drooling and shaking.

Marty: Actually, I would recommend putting you on the salad bar. Yep, no worries about drooling & shaking then.

Rick: Would you drown me in fat-free French dressing?

Marty: Yep, that would happen.

Rick: Enough talk of business. Soon I'll need to get back to the tasks at hand, sweeping the kitchen floor, vacuuming the carpet and dusting the furniture. Then I'll finish the fun stuff like the laundry and the dishes.

Marty: That's the way to do it. Save the fun stuff for last, something to look forward to! Hugs & Kisses!

Rick: Promise?

Marty: Yep.

Rick: Yessss! I've still got it. You could hear me cheering if it wasn't for that clanking dishwasher, the loose change bouncing around in the clothes dryer, and the stove timer.

Marty: You're still a multi-tasker.

Rick: Yes ma'am, I'm baking brownies too, the macho kind, no sprinkles, no chocolate chips. I ate those separately.

Marty: Umm umm good.

Rick: I'm pleased that you accepted my friend invitation on Facebook. I sent Cora a friend request. After a week with no response, I opened her site, approved myself, and sent me a provocative posting in her name. I bet my seven friends were jealous.

Marty: I read that over-the-top note. I couldn't help but giggle a bit.

Rick: Swell. This morning before "work" I went on a 20-mile bike ride. Now I'm trying to decide on how to reward myself, a tall glass of white wine or a homemade chocolate, banana, root beer milkshake. My doctor says that wine will over-stimulate my heart and ice cream will clog my arteries. Because I've persevered 40 years married to a blonde, blue-eyed, purebred, Norwegian babe and my blood pressure remains low, I'll have one of each.

Marty: Have one of each for me too.

Rick: Did you know that I'm celebrating my 40th wedding anniversary to Cora the Dish? I'm not sure what she's doing.

Marty: Congrats to you anyway. Have you been staying busy?

Rick: Yes, I have. You know how much I enjoy garage sales.

Marty: Sure do.

Rick: One recent Saturday morning, I nudged Cora and said "It's time to wake up. All the good, garage-sale junk will be gone." Cora replied in a stern yet drowsy voice, "Keep it up and your junk will be gone too."

Marty: How insensitive of her.

Rick: Yeah. I'm mourning the end of the garage-sale season. Goodbye great buys on stuff that I don't need and special purchases for my relatives and friends that are the wrong size, color, fashion, or considered in plain poor taste that they accept with a smile and a sideways glance, then donate to the hospice center. Until next year, I bid thee adieu.

Marty: I'm sad for you.

Rick: Don't be sad. I did find some outstanding buys this year even though I have yet to come across an authentic antique like they do on TV shows such as Antiques Roadshow and American Pickers. I mentioned something similar to Cora and she suggested that I bring a mirror.

Marty: You must admit that she's witty.

Rick: Swell. At times, I try to even the score with her but to no avail. Earlier this year when the clouds blocked the full eclipse of the moon, I performed an unobstructed similar spectacle for Cora's enjoyment. She said, "My tides didn't stir. That wasn't celestial. Now behave yourself."

Marty: How unromantic on her part.

Rick: Yeah, she just doesn't understand that behaving is not in my jeans.

Marty: Oh, she doesn't?

Rick: Thanks for the support. This morning I reminded Cora that I'll be 62 this month. Proactively, I stated, "I'm not old because I look to future adventures more than I do to past memories. I still feel young within." Cora replied: "Enjoy it. That's the only feel you're going to get."

Marty: _____

Rick: And that's not all. She followed up with, "I can imagine you singing, 'Happy birthday to me. Happy birthday to me. I made it past 60. I've got to go pee.'"

Once again Marty offered no reply, but I conjectured a snicker on her part.

Rick: And, and, when it rained yesterday, Cora encouraged our three-year-old grandson Grasyn to sing; "It's raining, it's pouring, the Old Man is snoring."

Marty: Oh, the youth of today.

Rick: Last night, Grasyn exclaimed, "I'm watching Looney Tunes."

Cora asked Grasyn: "Are you watching TV or Grandpa?"

Marty: ☺

Rick: The other day when I dropped my cell phone into the toilet, I borrowed Cora's phone. I think she programmed my number to go directly to voicemail.

Marty: You can do that? In-ter-es-ting.

Rick: They did it on a TV sitcom.

Marty: Well, that settles it.

Rick: Since Cora became head of household, most all the snail mail is addressed to her. The only mailings I receive are from AARP. An article in their latest self-titled magazine said that if you want to know who you are, ask your family and friends. I'm so screwed.

Marty: Calm down, Enrico.

Rick: Ok. I'll change the subject. I've enjoyed working on our forested land this past summer. I've cleared vast groves of thorny, botanical invasive species. The plants lost their lives but managed to vaccinate me on a regular basis. I should be immune from the flu, black plague, toe fungus, HPV, and Snookie.

When I return home from a typical day, Cora gathers her surgical instruments and dons her scrubs, latex gloves, and zippered, black-leather mask. She insists that I remain still while she removes thorns from my non-anesthetized body parts. The Dish enjoys the procedure just a little too much.

Marty: Ouch.

Rick: On the first Tuesday night of October, I mentioned to Cora about the excellent weather forecast for the month. Cora replied, "As a rule I've asked you to head out to your land on

Thursday and return home Tuesday night in time to take out the garbage for Wednesday morning pickup, and then head back out to your land again Thursday morning. Considering the perfect weather, you should leave tomorrow after the garbage pickup and return November 1st in time to sign your retirement check, and too late to scare the neighborhood kids on Halloween."

Marty: She's got a point.

Rick: Swell. To continue, a while back Cora bought me a trail camera because our land locale is well known for wildlife and a popular deer hunting destination. I posted it near my campsite where our neighbors Glen and Eric thought I might capture pictures of deer, badgers, coyotes, and black bears. I'm going to have to find a new spot to dance naked with the butterflies.

Marty: So you're a closet hippy. I bet Cora would get some mileage out of that.

Rick: She has. I'm certain she rigged the camera's Wi-Fi feature to feed directly to her laptop. Lord only knows what she'll do with those pictures. On a strange side note, the last time I was camping, I found my tent flap coated with bacon grease and a dozen doughnuts in the firewood pile.

Marty: The coyotes and bears have to eat too.

Rick: That's what she said. Earlier today via email, my neighbor Glen reported, "I saw two nice doe in my backyard. I could hunt from my porch. No, I want a trophy buck."

I replied, "You could ask the two doe to heat up the area to attract a trophy buck. If they're Norwegian doe, they'll finish him off for you and gut him too. Oh, is that unkind?"

Marty: Cora's NOT at home right now is she?

Rick: Nope. We're leaving on vacation early tomorrow morning to visit her sister Bev at her hobby farm in Joice, Iowa. They don't have the Internet so I'll have at least a week to enjoy life.

Marty: Or so you think.

Rick: Last summer when we visited Bev, Cora asked her, "As long as we're here, what say we add Rick to your compost heap?"
Bev countered, "He'd wreck the pH level."
Cora added, "He'd enhance the BS level."

Marty: Sisters forever.

Rick: Swell. On the first morning of our last vacation, Cora's work alarm blared unexpectedly. Cora reached over shut if off and said, "It's time for sex."

I replied enthusiastically, "I'm up for that."

To which Cora said, "What?" So I repeated her comment.

Through her laughter, she corrected me by stating, "I said it's ten till six."

Marty: Just a simple misunderstanding.

Rick: Yeah. Now though, I blurt out, it's ten till six, whenever I can work it into the conversation. Every time I earn a crack on the head or at least a sideways glance.

Marty: By now you should've learned to stay out of her reach.

Rick: I suppose so. Yesterday I got another crack on the head for this, simple misunderstanding, which I plan to post on Facebook:

I had made a comment to Cora about something or other and she answered, "Ah, Bah-low-nee."

I answered immediately in disbelief, "Did you say, ah blow me?"

Her firm denial accompanied a crack on the head. I'm donning my hard hat as soon as I activate the post button.

Marty: Uh, oh.

Kristin, our daughter-in-law, rudely barged in on our Facebook conversation. I believe it's fair for me to say that she is in cahoots with Cora. I've come to the conclusion that women rule the earth. At least the patch I live on.

Kristin: So you think she won't find out about your Facebook posts huh?

Rick: No, not right away, unless someone squeals.

Marty: Ah, Facebook has been keeping families together for eight years now.

Kristin: I'm thinking you should find your bike helmet before Cora gets home.

Rick: Find my bike helmet? Skull protection is the least of my worries.

Rick: Marty, I think my sons are in league with Cora too.

Marty: Now why would you think that?

Rick: A couple years ago one of them signed me up with Bed Wetters Anonymous. I got informative mailings and meeting notifications until just recently when I could have actually used them. Two weeks ago, one of the boys booked me an appointment and two follow up visits at a beauty salon for a Brazilian waxing. The zombies in Dante's 7th hell would hear me screaming.

Marty: Sounds like something Cora would enjoy witnessing.

Rick: With that thought in mind, it's off I am to complete my man's work. Cora will be home from her job at 6:16 p.m., and I need to prepare dinner and freshen up a bit. See ya.

Marty: My best to Cora. Bye.

Rick: Swell.

#####

THE 3H CLUB

I've found, since my retirement began, twelve years distant, that the titled position of Humble House Husband carries but few benefits. Other tenured members of this club, I'm sure, have found yourselves to be equally disadvantaged, overworked, underappreciated, bereft of a secret handshake.

I've acquired diverse skills, a few by trial and error, most by impatient, after-the-fact instruction from Cora, my wife, head of household, even a few, thanks to Oprah. In the rough draft of this story, I misspelled Oprah as Opera. Based upon the pack of sniveling whiners on her show, such would've been apropos.

As a veteran of this unsought post, I'd like to offer the following tutorial for recent draftees. Hopefully, this hard-earned wisdom will save you from the occasional ass-chewing, sideways glance, libelous Facebook comment, and slanderous remark at wifey gatherings.

(I just received an ass-chewing for accusing Cora of ass-chewing, and then another ass-chewing for writing ass-chewing in this story.)

Yearly, we host our extended family's Thanksgiving dinner. Cora prepares cookies, puddings, pies, fruit salad, cake, and Rice Krispie bars, accompanied by incidentals such as turkey, stuffing, and mashed potatoes.

As I'm not involved in the prep work, I'm expected to handle the cleanup. A word of warning, if by any chance you're unaware: remove the sacrosanct items from the washables. I mistakenly scrubbed a stack of cookie sheets, cake pans, and Cora's esteemed coffee cup. OMG, it was Armageddon. My mismanagement removed several layers of the seasoned crud so important to the final flavor of cookies, cakes, and coffee. I trust that Cora will remember this incident the next time she dines from one of our savory dinner plates.

II

To my credit, I've become a self-proclaimed laundry maven. I'm careful to sort all the clothing, as instructed, if Cora is home, before it becomes soap-spotted within the water-conserving washing machine, and wrinkled beyond recognition in the 31-setting dryer.

I'm not talking about sorting by patterns but rather by ranges of color: white, sort-of-white, dark-white, colored, dark, almost-dark, and light-dark. All colors and non-colors, except white, should not be bleached with bleach but instead color-safe-bleach, which I conjecture is expensive soap.

Thanks to creative sorting, I'm able to produce a multicolored, abstract work of art in the lint trap. I'll retain the exact means of that process until my patent application is approved.

Lingerie must be washed with the gentle cycle. It doesn't hold up well with the same setting as blue jeans. That's counterintuitive. I don't treat lingerie gently while Cora is so adorned. Okay, you're right. I don't get to treat lingerie in any fashion while she's so adorned.

Similarly, the "underthings" must be dried via the gentle cycle or be gently draped upon the shower rod, the edge of the bathtub, and the little hooks on the closet door.

Of what value is lacey, amorphous underwear if I'm not allowed to admire Cora while she's so adorned? Screw gentle.

III

There's a fine art to sweeping, vacuuming and dusting...in that order. Sweep all hard services, then vacuum the same to suck up all microscopic spider turds that have evaded the broom bristles.

Vacuuming the carpet is the next step. All furniture and hearing aids must first be removed before activating "the beast." No matter what type of carpet you have, it has a grain; find it and vacuum against it. In some ways, that's similar to what I manage to do with Cora, daily, unintentionally.

Lastly, dusting is last. That way you can remove most of the dust that the vacuum cleaner flung around the house. And by the way, use a microfiber cloth, not wet rags or lingerie. And, and don't shake out the cloth on the front stoop while the door is open.

IV

The following is a partial list of lessons learned, most of which earned me a butt chomping, what little was left of it:

- Remove coins, candy, cell phones, combs, pocket knives, ink pens and fish baits from your pants pockets before washing.

- Lingerie does not care to be cleaned in the company of forestry garb. One displaced thorn or wood tick can be (is) life-threatening.

- Use a paper towel to dry real-bleach wetted fingers, not your jeans.

- Fake fur, leather, and down jackets don't wash well.

- Turn the dryer on after you fill it.

- While vacuuming, avoid Legos, marbles, screws, nuts, paper clips, and Hershey's kisses.

- Pitch plastic utensils into the wastebasket, not the dishwasher.

- There isn't a dishwasher dead or alive that can clean a chili pot.

- Knives should be pointed downward when loaded into the utensils port.

- When cleaning toilets, avoid springy bristled brushes, and flush before your wife makes use of their services.

- A woman's women's magazines are sacred.
- Of most importance, all chores, of any kind, must be completed while the wife is away and out of cell phone range.

While incommunicado, I wish 3H-Club inductees health and happiness because you will own humility.

#####

QUIPS AND QUOTES

Cora and I exchanged anniversary gifts:
I gave her flowers.
She hired the neighbor's son to mow our lawn.

Cora watches a TV show about a guy with four wives. He must be freakin' nuts!

After our kids moved out on their own, the cat disappeared, the dog died and the goldfish got flushed, Cora promoted me to Vice President of our household. It's an honorary position.

On one of our early dates, being the spendthrift that I was, am, Cora Sue Johnson and I stopped at a Kentucky Fried Chicken. I offered, "Order whatever you want." Country girl ordered a jumbo package of deep-fried chicken gizzards.

Almost right counts as a victory for husbands.

I get up before sunrise and leave the lights off so that I don't wake Cora. I have done well except for this morning while brushing my teeth, the sink seemed mighty low.

I worked long and hard to earn my immaturity.

I'm old enough so that I don't have to make excuses for my sense of humor.

###

MY FEAT

As I sit here at the computer, I take a shallow bow, carefully. In true fumbling, family fashion, I have bested my father's, famed feats. During a home repair project, while standing on a wheeled, ladder-back chair, I managed to stumble and plunge an entire 18 inches onto the dehumidifier. The appliance rejected my advances and cast me down onto the concrete floor below, breaking the same bones in both of my feet.

Therefore, I've received from the doctoral staff at the local medical clinic, a set of plastic-pillared, King Kong boots complete with internal, pneumatic cushions, senior-citizen socks that shinny all the way up to the fork-in-the-road, an appointment with a bone surgeon, pleasant, pitying smiles, and a bottle of pills that would sedate the aforementioned ape, who by the way, would not wish to have his name mentioned in the same sentence or story as mine. Please forgive the previous run-on sentence as it may be my only opportunity to run for a while.

Tomorrow, I'm scheduled to visit a foreign-national surgeon who in all probability had his life savings tied up in American, subprime-mortgage, bond clusters and real-estate L.L.C.s. He is certain to apply casts that will cover most of my person except for access and egress ports. I will be punctured with various pins and screws enabling me to perform Spock's Vulcan salutation with both fingers and toes simultaneously.

Prior to my crack-up, I had challenged my sons to a 110-mile, one-day bicycle trek. Though unspoken, they've inferred that I wimped out.

I'm currently planning a space-age refit of my bicycle in the hallowed tradition of the original *Star Trek* that will allow me to once again throw down the gauntlet and stumble over it.

Live long and prosper _\\ //

SWEET PREDILECTION

I have a predilection for sweets, just to name a few: all flavors of ice cream and cookies with the exception of those infused with heart-healthy nuts; sugar-coated breakfast cereals with the exception of Kellogg's Frosted Mini-Wheats due to its heart-healthy, whole-grain ingredient, and candy, no exceptions, even the infamous crown-cracking candy categories.

I'm not to blame. While I was growing up, my mother, bless her heart, baked, baked, and baked some more—everything and anything that contained mostly sugar. I should've been an 800-pound toddler. Instead, my inability to sleep, incoherent babbling, chewed-to-the-quick fingernails, and the constant running in circles, wore off the calories before my next serving, much to my mother's chagrin. She never did figure out the cause of my hyperactivity.

Grandma Wehler, while babysitting, served steaming Quaker Oats for breakfast. After she left the kitchen, I sprinkled sugar on the oatmeal and it disappeared. So I sprinkled on more with the same result. Over and over again. When she returned, my eyes were the size of silver dollars as I poured the remainder of the sugar bowl's contents onto the last scoop of oatmeal. Unfamiliar with hot breakfast cereal, I just didn't know that sugar melted and disappeared.

She smiled and replaced my empty cereal bowl with another serving. My uncle Bobby, just a few years older than I, refilled the sugar bowl. Once again, I bathed my oatmeal. I gobbled the first spoonful and gagged. Grandma came running in at the sound of my distress and found that Uncle Bobby had mistakenly filled the sugar bowl with salt. To this day, I sample first.

Not much has changed over the years. My frame has remained slim. I sleep sometimes, sort of. I'm an awe-inspiring runamouth after meals. I haven't owned a fingernail in my entire life. And, the circle running has expanded to such a degree that some have blamed dark matter.

I've earned all of my 69 years, and I've begun to reflect upon my sweet predilection. Recently, I noticed that Tony the Tiger, my lifetime breakfast companion, is toothless. Soon Tony and I will have something in common besides breakfast.

While in search of bird food at the newly opened Fleet Farm store, famous for pet foods, garden-ware, and farm implements, I found a display of Nut Goodie candy bars, a product normally unavailable in Wisconsin. I selected a dozen or so. Another display contained bags of sour cherry balls. I picked up a few of those. I returned to the front of the store to grab a shopping cart and continued my search. My bill was less than $100 once I returned the birdseed to the display.

The first two Nut Goodies tasted grrrreat! Four more grace my candy jar, and the remainder are in the freezer as backup in case of the zombie apocalypse.

I noticed that the first handful of sour cherries tasted too sweet. I checked the ingredients labels and, and f-f-found no fault, as sugar was listed first in every case. I surmised that this batch contained 99 percent sugar and 1 percent sour instead of 97 percent sugar and 3 percent sour. I fed them to the grandkids.

The grocery store, where I work part-time, had a grocery cart overflowing with two-and-a-half-pound bags of Brach's Candy Corn, the good stuff, marked down from $7.99 to 50 cents! I've already given two bags to our son Andy, and I'm in deep doo-doo with his wife Kristin. As I still have a hidden stash of more than I'm allowed to own under any circumstances, I gave a bag to the neighbor kids. The rest I'm keeping no matter what anybody says. I asked my wife Cora if I could buy the entire cart full and then hand out a bag to each kid next Halloween, if there's any remaining. NOPE. Ap-parent-ly she values the mothers.

My predilection for sweets continues. In the future, if I have one, for such incredible deals, I'll rent a locker at the Walking Dead's cold storage plant.

#####

WHAT?

Recently, over the past three years, Cora has encouraged me repeatedly to invest in a set of high-tech hearing aids. I don't feel the need. She enjoys interacting with the congregation, and I'm grateful for my inability to do so. I've improved at reading her lips, certain words in particular.

We visited the hearing-services department at the UW Health Medical Center in mid-October. After an evaluation, Jen, the audiologist, stated, "Your hearing sucks." I lip-read "sucks," having become familiar with that descriptor and its derivations recently.

Jen handed us a one-page, hearing-aid, price listing: Ultimate grade, $6,600/pair; Mid-level, $4,800/pair; and Standard, $3,400/pair. I flipped the listing over and found Basic, $1,800/pair, all by itself. Those prices are for the models that hang loose. The molded, ear-canal versions are an additional $700/pair. I'm confident that Jen had no problem hearing my reaction. Cora didn't. I read her lips.

I convinced both women to grant me a few days to consider the selection.

Dwane, a Facebook friend, my normal investigative site, posted that he'd purchased effective hearing aids from the Costco in Charlotte, NC at a much cheaper price. I'm not a shopper and thought of Costco in terms of rotisserie chicken, blueberry muffins, and XL boxes of WetWipes.

I mentioned Dwane's recommendation to Cora. She verified that our local Costco has a Hearing Aid department located next to the Health and Beauty aisle.

We set up an appointment for the following week.

The Hearing Instrument Specialist, probably a graduate of a six-month, online course at a for-profit college, Derek Doze, yawned continually as he explained the computerized tests. As Jen did at UW Health, he placed a probe within each of my ears and

WHAT?

ran through a series of beeps. I needed only to push a button when I heard a beep. I thought, "I can do this. I'm familiar with bleeps when I push Cora's buttons."

The following test, with probes in place, asked me to repeat computer-spoken words. I found that challenging without the lips, but made it through with few mistakes, much to Cora's surprise. He then, between yawns, removed the probes and secured speakers to my skull. I asked him to reposition them, twice, as his attempts landed them on a few of the lumps Cora raised after I passed the spoken-words test.

Derek presented me with a printout of the tests' results. In agreement with Jen, the hearing in my right ear sucks and my left ear sucks less. He then handed me a list of their prices: Premium, $2,500/pair and the store brand, Kirkland, $1,599/pair. I flipped over the page and found the backside blank. The UW Health prices were much more to my disliking.

Later, at home, Cora and I reasoned that even if Costco's premium hearing aids don't measure up to the UW's ultimate, we could compare them to the UW's mid-level and still pay $2,300 less. I relented and ordered the Costco premium hearing aids.

A week later, Derek Doze fitted my equipment, nearly puncturing my right ear drum during a yawn. I'm confident that he had no problem hearing my reaction.

Per his instructions, I'd downloaded the hearing-aid app onto my smartphone. Doze programmed my hearing aids, connected them to the app, and gave me a one-minute tutorial. I'm now able to control the volume and all of the applications from my smartphone or tap out the Morse code instructions on the hearing aids themselves.

Each aid is labeled with a miniscule, colored, identity patch: blue for the left ear and red for the right ear. I can't see the patches. Demonstrating uncommon intelligence, I've learned to recognize left from right by the angle of the probes.

It's the week of Halloween, and I've discovered that hearing aids have a dark side—I'm hearing voices.

#####

AFTERTHOUGHTS

I received a Medicare video on prevention of vision loss but I couldn't hear it.

###

My hearing aids are installed. Goodbye peace and tranquility.

###

Hearing aids should scream for help, not drown silently in the bathtub.

###

The tech said, "It may take up to six months for your brain to adjust to the hearing aids."
 I replied, "Meh, It's taken 47 years and six months to adjust to marriage...so far."

###

Two days with my hearing aids, and I don't think I've missed much without them.

###

I've had my hearing aids for a month, worn them for ten days, and Cora has found them, not surprisingly, ineffective.

###

Thank you, $2,500 hearing aids. Now I can still distinguish no words at all, even louder.

###

My hearing aids didn't seem to be making a difference so I turned up the volume, significantly. Cellophane crackles loudly, a sneeze nearly blows my brains out, and while relaxing with a good book, I can hear my mind reading.

###

WHAT?

I'm brushing my teeth and don't have the hearing aids turned on when Cora walks into the bathroom and says, "I'm going on a drive for the dealership, so I won't be getting naked."

I shot back, "Forget the drive!"

She said, "What?"

So I repeated what I heard her say.

I got "the look" and Cora said, "I said, 'I'm going on a drive for the dealership, so the cookies won't be getting bake-ed.'"

I said, "Forget the drive."

###

Tonight, after Cora and I found a TV show that we were willing to watch together, I set the TV's volume at 21. Cora ordered that I don the headset speakers over my hearing aids. As I did so, she reset the TV's volume to 7.

###

HUBCAP

On May 31, 1991, I set up a plan to retire on May 31, 2007. I'd confidently followed the plan, feeling good about my progress, until the 2001 dot.com debacle. Although heartsick, I stuck with the plan and didn't sell our investments.

February 2004, while on a road trip to my employer's grocery store in Beloit, Wisconsin, I was feeling mighty low, fearing that I wasn't going to make my retirement goal. Suddenly, I hit a pothole on the freeway and lost a hubcap. That was the last straw. I turned around, went home, and told my wife Cora Sue that all was lost.

Cora Sue insisted that we retrace my route to Beloit. As we approached town, she asked me to take a best guess as to where I lost the hubcap. I remembered a bridge that passed over the freeway not far from a frontage-road gas station. She pulled into the median, parked, and ordered me to get out of the car to begin a ticket-worthy search and rescue.

Right there, RIGHT THERE, as I opened the passenger door, lay my hubcap. How did she do it?

I can't explain why I was broken-hearted at losing a lousy hubcap or elated at finding it. Cora Sue saved my hubcap and my resolve to retire.

At age 57½, right on time, I became a retired dude. I climbed aboard my Trek bicycle and went on a long ride through the countryside. Never had I felt so free.

I've enjoyed 12 years of retirement thus far. Recently, 20 minutes after returning from another bicycle ride, my heart went freaking nuts.

HUBCAP

After three hours of tests, the emergency room doc prescribed a heart medication and sent me home.

I stopped by the Walmart pharmacy to pick it up.

The clerk said, "That will be 91…"

I interrupted, "Dollars?!!!."

She finished, "Cents."

I mumbled, "Heart, just another hubcap."

#####

I'LL BE BACK

As I nestled into my man-cave recliner with the heating pad maxed out, I listened to *La Traviata* on the CD player and drifted into a world of memories about our three sons, Jerry, Andy, and Toby.

We ventured out onto the cement driveway during a summer rain. Jerry sporting an umbrella. Andy and Toby each with a garbage can lid held high for shelter. Such a feeling of safety when all else is drenched. I carried an empty ice cream pail as we walked along the paved surface, thumbs and forefingers unreservedly harvesting slimy angle worms for fish bait.

II

I told a juvenile joke at the dinner table. Jerry's knowing smile accompanied Andy's bewildered countenance. Toby expelled his mouthful of food, buckled, fell to the floor, and rolled beneath the table beset by laughter. We all roared in accompaniment, grasping our sides rather than the punch line.

III

Toby drenched in perspiration, ten seconds ahead of the junior high school, basketball playoff-game's final buzzer, receives a pass from the sidelines. His jump shot from the beyond the foul line, swish, victory!

IV

Jerry, introspective, a thinker, shares with Cora and me after a 10th-grade field trip that he's going to become a software-design engineer. He devoted himself to that end and had three job offers months before graduating from college with honors.

"Jerry, why don't you accept a job where you've been working during school."

"Dad, I can do better."

You did do better.

V

The guys all took on Tae Kwon Do. Jerry, serious and concentrating on every move. Andy breaking boards without a problem. Toby, joking his way through with invented karate dance moves. Within two years, Andy, age eleven, and Toby, age nine, earned black belts. Jerry, age fifteen, per his goal, dropped out one rank shy to pursue a black belt in computer electronics.

VI

The boys were seated about the backyard, hilltop, campfire hollow, beneath the shimmering box elder trees, engaged in a much-loved, summer-night delight: roasting marshmallows. Cora and I crashed through the back door as the sounds of merriment transformed into cries of terror. We raced up the rise as Jerry's silhouette rescued Toby from the fire pit. Snatching Toby from Jerry's arms, I rushed him towards the house, brushing glowing embers from his bare palms and knees while comforting, "You can stop screaming. You're safe." He quieted.

After first aid, Cora inquired, "Where are the other boys?" Andy was still at the fire pit, crying, while Jerry paced the patio, head bowed, overwhelmed.

VII

Andy and his lady at a high school dance; some guy makes a comment about his girl. Andy puts on his karate, kick-ass face and the guy disappears into the crowd.

"Rick, are you alive in there?" Cora teased from the ether.

Evidently, that's enough reminiscing for today.

The boys are grown up and fashioning their own lives. I miss them.

I'll be back.

#####

BANTER BATTLES

"Cora, as I remember, you're the best lover I've ever had."

"Rick, I'm the only lover you've ever had."

"Dish, I'm waiting. You're supposed to say the same about me."

"Hubber, you're the only lover I've ever had. Could be the best. Could be the worst."

###

"Cora, this article says that those who swear can expect to be more mentally healthy than those who don't."

"Hubber, it's been 70 years for you. How long until it takes effect?"

###

"Cora, let's go out on a dinner date tonight."

"Okay, Hubber, but there will be five changes, maybe six: you choose the place, make the reservation, drive, order the meal, pay for it, and maybe you can hope for six."

###

After all of our extended family went home I commented, "Cora, I like having you for my girlfriend. We should go steady."

She replied, "Okay, but I'm still not putting out."

###

"Wifey, for our 47th wedding anniversary, I'll take you out to dinner. But, I want a commitment for three more years of marriage."

She countered, "Hubber, one year of probation."

I replied, "Deal!"

###

49

"Hubber, you've lost your humor filters over the years. I read your Facebook posts."

"Wifey, it's age-related."

"Hubber, you're not getting any younger, and if this keeps up, you're not getting any older."

I inquired, "You have a lace bra? I'd love to see it."

Cora replied, "It's in the laundry basket."

As I raised my pajama pant leg to put on socks Cora commented. "You're showing some leg."

I replied, "It hasn't worked in 48 years, but I'm not giving up hope."

"Cora, I'm chilly this morning."

"Hubber, I gave you the cold shoulder."

"Wifey, it's better than nothing."

I snuck into the bathroom while Cora was in the shower, admired the view, and hollered, "I see you."

She wrote in the steam on the glass shower door: I.C.U."

I left the area.

###

Long Odds

Today, I'm in the mood to play the long odds. I might just get lucky. With that in mind, I'm submitting the following query to the *Car Talk* newspaper columnists expecting that they will make use of it in their publication.

Dear Tom and Ray,

Ms. Penny Purebred, my tan 1997 Ford Taurus, and I have a time-honored, symbiotic relationship: I tend to her upkeep and she gets me where I want to go. A time or two, I neglected to check her oil level. Ms. Purebred burns a bit of oil between changes due to her advancing age. (I hope that she doesn't read your column.) On each occasion, she alerted me of my oversight by dropping her fuel efficiency from 27 mpg to 25 mpg or less, depending upon the depth of my thoughtlessness. Is there a relationship between oil level and fuel efficiency or is she just being persnickety?

I might just as well throw caution into the slipstream and pose a second question. When I apply Penny's brakes by pressing firmly mid-pedal, she responds most admirably. If I lazily move my foot from her accelerator to the edge of her brake pedal, she squeals like a girl of much younger years. Should I be scolded or she?

Thanks,
Rick Wehler

#####

51

A BORROWED, BLACK 1958
FORD THUNDERBIRD

PREFACE

I t took a while to write this story about a 1958 fishing trip with my father and his friend because I had to rely on my memory. When a thought popped in, I'd write it down before I forgot it. Later, during moments of clarity, I'll separate fact from fiction.

Today, I decided it's unlikely that Marilyn Monroe came along, and the wind on the lake blew her skirt up.

###

Dad: Ricky, it's time to get up.

Ricky: It's still dark.

Dad: Get up. Frosty will be here soon.

It was 4:30 a.m. on a July morning in 1958. Dad and his best friend, Frosty Williams, both 30 years old, had borrowed a black 1958 Ford Thunderbird from the Minneapolis car dealership where they worked as salesmen.

Dad: Ricky, we're heading to the Canadian border fishing and camping. It's a long drive. We've got to get going.

I was excited to be included in the trip even though at eight years old, I'd never been fishing or camping. I downed two bowls of cereal while Dad and Frosty loaded a holstered pistol, a bottle of liquor, and other contraband into the Thunderbird's excuse for a trunk.

I sat in the backseat of the modern sports car while Dad and Frosty occupied the front bucket seats that were separated by a center console with a built-in ashtray. I didn't question the lack of fishing and camping gear.

Before I knew it, we were cruising due north on a two-lane highway, leaving Minneapolis well behind. I gazed at the long, flat, empty road ahead in the early morning light from between the bucket seats and through the Marlboro cigarette smog that filled the cabin.

Dad: Ricky, read the speedometer.

I rubbed my stinging eyes, looked over his shoulder and read, "104!"

> **Dad:** That's right. This machine can fly!
> **Frosty:** It's starting to float.

Dad laughed and slowed down a bit.

Sometime later, we left the paved roads well behind too. Up ahead, the horizon was far off; the sky, pale blue. The scattered clouds reminded me of Mom's mashed potatoes, without the gravy.

Dad turned off the main dirt road and meandered through many a bumpy, wooded, back road until we arrived at a lodge on the southern end of Crane Lake. Dad had reserved a tipsy aluminum boat with a beat-up motor, filled with enough fishing and camping gear to keep it steady on the big lake.

We motored along close to the rocky, inlet-strewn shoreline until we entered the Little Vermilion Straits on the Minnesota/Canadian border. We followed the strait until Frosty pointed and said, "There's the island dead ahead." As we approached he commented, "Oh, someone's already camping there. We'll have to find another spot."

Dad followed Frosty's directions until they spotted a rock outcropping bordered by trees that jutted into the strait. We pulled up onto shore at dusk and unloaded the gear. Dad and Frosty erected a floorless, canvas tent, unrolled army blankets, set up a campfire pit, uncorked a bottle of booze, poured a little into two camping cups, and handed me a warm bottle of Bubble-Up.

We sat by the campfire and looked out over the water as the full moon's reflection stretched across the strait, bouncing on the waves. Even at my age, I was stunned by the beauty. We donned our lack of swimming suits and floated on the waves within the moon's reflection.

I slept soundly on the rocky ground wrapped in an army blanket.

The next morning Dad said, "You woke in the middle of the night, sat up, pointed at the tent door, and screamed 'a bear!' Frosty and I jumped out from under our blankets, and Frosty unholstered his Ruger pistol. There was no bear, so we all settled back down."

That was news to me.

We hiked up into the woods and found a border marker between the two countries: left foot in the U.S.A., right foot in Canada.

Later that morning, after a breakfast of scrambled eggs and bacon, we climbed aboard the now-roomy aluminum boat and headed out hunting for a fishing spot. Dad and Frosty had purchased a few dozen sucker minnows as bait. We stopped at a likely spot and Frosty gave me some fishing instructions.

Frosty: Ricky, this is a casting rod and reel. See this hook? I'll stick a minnow on it. Good. Now put the rod over the edge of the boat, let the reel spin and the line sink to the bottom. You'll know because the reel will stop spinning. Then crank until the count of three and stop. We're fishing for walleye. So you'll see the rod tip pulled down a little when they're nibbling. The third time the rod tip goes down, put your thumb on the reel and pull back hard. You'll know if you have something. Then just start cranking the handle.

We didn't have any luck that morning and headed back to camp. As I sat on the shore eating my peanut butter and jelly sandwich, I fished with my rod lying on the ground, holding the line in my hand, and dipping the hooked minnow into the water. Minutes later, I saw a giant head reach for the minnow. I pulled in the line and the head disappeared. I couldn't imagine what it was. I yelled, "Dad, Dad, come here, hurry."

Dad and Frosty ran over expecting a problem.

Ricky: Dad, there's a giant head down there.

Dad: Dip your bait in again.

Sure enough, up came the head. Frosty ran to the tent and returned with his Ruger pistol. He took careful aim with the pistol in his right hand resting on his raised left elbow, and fired at the head. It disappeared and didn't come back, so we returned to camp.

After lunch, I looked toward the shore, and there was a giant snapping turtle crawling along the rocky shore with a blood trail behind it. Frosty came up, took his shooting stance, and shot it again, twice.

Frosty: That's a monster. It'd make for a great dinner.

Ricky: You can eat those?

Dad: Sure, if we had a pot big enough to cook it.

Frosty picked it up and pitched it into the lake.

We climbed aboard the boat, leaving the fishing gear behind, to do some site-seeing. Dad, up front, spotted a loon, and with Frosty at the tiller, we gave chase. That loon turned on a dime, several times, and Frosty did much the same with our shallow-hulled boat while Dad reached forward with the landing net. We all shouted with excitement, including the loon that finally gave us the bird, dove beneath the surface and escaped.

Late afternoon, near a big rock that stuck up out of the water, we found a good fishing spot. Dad and Frosty caught a few nice-sized walleyes. Then I had my first bite. I did just as Frosty instructed: let the rod bounce three times and pulled back hard. I had one. I just kept cranking as the rod bent into an upside-down U and jumped to and fro.

Dad yelled, "I've got the net. Slide your rod this way."

Together we boated my first fish ever!

We caught several walleyes in that spot and then headed to camp. Dad and Frosty cleaned the fish and fried them over the campfire in a big iron skillet, sizzling with the bacon grease that Frosty had saved from breakfast. Never, ever, in my life had I tasted anything so delicious. What a change from our meals at home that consisted of anything cheap, especially mashed potatoes.

That night went by peacefully, no bear sightings, and we were out early, fishing on our hot spot. We caught several walleyes once again but disaster struck. The stringer broke loose from the boat and sunk to the bottom with all of our catch.

Dad had always been a top-notch swimmer, a competitor as a teenager. He could still swim three lengths of the pool at the YMCA underwater without taking a breath. Dad stripped down, not feeling the need for a swimsuit in the wilderness, and dove all around the boat, celebrating as he surfaced, by holding the stringer of fish high above the water.

I continued to follow the successful fishing technique I'd learned from Frosty. *Wham!* No three rod jiggles, just *wham!* I jerked my rod back, it slammed forward and bent over the edge of the boat. I tried to reel but the reel wouldn't reel.

Frosty: Ricky, it's ok; wait a minute. When the line goes slack a bit, then reel.

I followed his advice and within a few minutes, the biggest fish I'd ever seen broke the surface. The water splashed as it struggled; first on its left side, then flipping over and diving again. It was a ways away from the boat as it fought. I reeled and reeled.

Frosty: Play it, Ricky.

I didn't know what that meant and kept reeling. The fish jumped into the sky, flopped back down onto the waves, splashed like crazy, and bit through my line. My rod jumped backwards. I was afraid that I'd done something wrong.

Frosty: That's ok. It's not your fault. We should have put a wire leader on your line that the fish couldn't bite through.

Ricky: What kind of fish was that?

Frosty: A northern pike. They have really sharp teeth.

Ricky: How big was it?

Frosty: At least fifteen pounds, a monster. There's more of them out there and you have a wire leader. So go get'em.

No northerns, but we caught so many walleyes that we ran out of minnows.

Dad put a Marlboro butt on his hook, laughed, and sank it to the bottom. Immediately, he caught a fine walleye. Frosty still had a minnow on his line and landed a walleye at the same time. Dad and Frosty both slapped their catches and managed to get the fish to cough up half-eaten minnows, our new, successful bait.

We dined like kings again that night; stayed up late, after the moon set, and floated on our backs in the quiet waters beneath the unbelievable, swirling masses of color, pink, green, yellow and blue that are the Northern Lights.

The next morning, we packed up and headed home. On our return trip, I bathed in the memories of our adventure as we flew through space and time in a borrowed, black 1958 Ford Thunderbird.

#####

HYDRATE

At the conclusion of my recent emergency room stay, six hours was the long and short of it, the doc said, "Dehydration could lead to rapid, uncontrollable, heart beat and high blood pressure. If you're planning to work at your forested property again in this heat, be sure to hydrate."

I appreciated the advice and commented, "If so, sounds like I'd be putting my remaining kidney to good use."

I wasn't feeling much like working in the forest. I'd be in the company of squirrels, raccoons, foxes, bobcats, coyotes, buzzards, and the occasional bullfrog if I happened to croak from heart problems.

Six days later, having lived the time without heart complications, other than the odd beats in response to the $435, thirty-day supply of Eliquis, I decided to pack up and head out to our forested property, Westwoods. I brought along my work list, crammed with jobs that nature will disregard.

The weather forecast called for temps and humidity in the mid-80s. I donned the lightest, long-sleeve flannel shirt in my wardrobe, thick work pants that shield against unambitious thorns, and a ballcap emblazoned with a fishing lure and the epitaph, "Cranky Old Man." (I'm not a fisherman.) I stepped into unused, half-size-too-large, waterproof, work boots while adorned in a pair of thick, smart-wool socks to fill the void.

I packed a bag lunch including a turkey sandwich, lots of cookies, and to hydrate, a can of Dr. Pepper, accompanied by three one-quart canteens of water.

As I stepped out of my air-conditioned CRV at Westwoods, the oppressive heat and humidity punched me nearly as hard as a PO'ed Norwegian wifey. But, I've got my list of unnecessary projects to accomplish.

I strapped on the 30-pound backpack herbicide sprayer, and hiked about baptizing garlic mustard, a plant considered an invasive species. Years ago, it had escaped the gardens of those gourmands who planted it as a zesty salad ingredient, and spiced up forests and fields throughout southern Wisconsin. That completed, I downed a canteen of water, overcompensating for that which soaked through my clothing ... from sweat.

I moved on to my next task: weeding around the 300 sapling oak trees my gentle wifey and I had planted four years ago along Westwood's southern border, the stream that runs 24/7 along the eastern border, and in the Oak Forest Swamp, a two-acre, hidden, sundrenched valley, a veritable terrarium.

After completing the borders, I downed another canteen of water and hiked to the Oak Forest Swamp, The trees have grown much taller here, matched by the surrounding berry bushes, nettles and grasses, thanks to the waters that flow down the hillsides after a rain, the stream that cuts through their midst, and the unrelenting sunshine.

I downed another canteen of water.

Back at my campsite rest area, I traded my soaked, rude-smelling work clothing, and sodden waterproof boots for a wife-beater shirt, shorts, and tennies; popped the Dr. Pepper, climbed into my CRV, and chose the Antarctic setting on the air conditioner.

Twenty miles into the 80-mile trip home, I, I had to find a bathroom, a secluded tree, or volunteer one of my empty canteens. I turned off the main road, ventured through hamlets, and found unnamed gas stations with restrooms of a sort, pleased that I didn't have to sit down. I arrived home, left the car door ajar, and raced into the front-hall, half-bathroom.

While in the hot, humid forest, I drained three canteens and a Dr. Pepper attempting to hydrate. On the way home, I hydrated three redneck johns, and spent the air-conditioned overnight hours at home pissing off my kidney.

#####

QUIPS AND QUOTES

When Cora gets ticked off at some driver on the roadways, she's likely to call him a stoopnagle, a dweeb, or a dingleberry. All words that I'd never use.

I was thinking about installing a doorbell security camera, but then Cora would know that it's me at the door.

I told our sons, "On tough days, just remember what we taught you, because I don't."

When my books become a movie, Xena the Warrior Princess should portray Cora.

After 48 years of marriage, I'm now in charge of one thing and one thing only: Nothing! I accept the responsibility.

Our grandson Noah is an exotic-plant expert. At Westwoods, I'm a face-plant expert.

Even though we're rich, thanks to our Social Security checks, I still scrape the last bits out of the Miracle Whip and Skippy Peanut Butter jars, and I punish the toothpaste tube.

###

THREE-POUND TEST
AS TOLD BY ANDY WEHLER

Memorial Day morning, I decided to fish the Yahara River at Tenney Park in Madison, Wisconsin, for bluegills and white bass. In previous seasons, I'd caught a few white bass and my limit of gills many times. I set up an ultra-light rod-and-reel combo with a three-pound-test line and a one-inch-long, single-hooked, minnow lure. I chose a fishing spot beneath the E. Johnson Street bridge where the water flowed clear. That way I could spot the schools of fish swimming by.

It didn't take long to land twenty white bass, filling a 5-gallon bucket to the halfway point. This has been a strange season in that the white bass catch has greatly outnumbered the bluegill tally.

I said to no one in particular, "Hey, there's a musky." With nothing to lose, I whipped the bait just past him and jerked it back right in front of his nose. The little lure was either too tempting or it just ticked him off. He slammed it and took off down stream, tugging against my useless drag. As I stood and watched, I thought, "There goes all my line and 50-cent, garage-sale lure."

But the musky turned upstream and I managed to reel in a bit. He leaped out of the water like one of those humpback whales you see on the Nature Channel except that he flapped several times before splashing back into the water. He raced towards the far shore, turned downstream again and made another acrobatic leap.

Shortly after our battle began, the musky and I attracted an on-shore audience of a dozen or so fishermen and passersby, all cheering me on. A few complimented my calm demeanor. They couldn't hear the screams in my head or my pounding heart. A group of canoeists paddled by, avoided my line, and excitedly shouted size reports of the monster that fought just below their crafts.

The musky eventually began to tire and came close to shore for a rest, but bolted when I reached down to grab him. Several minutes later, he came near shore once again. I didn't have a net, so I stretched past the shore line and grabbed his back just behind the gills with my Vulcan death grip. I then slid my other hand underwater to his belly and caught him in the slot beneath his gills. I lifted him up and out of the water to the cheers of the shore crowd and the folks in the canoes.

This was no ordinary musky, but a beautifully patterned tiger musky. I didn't find a DNR survey tag on its gill plates, but his scars made it look as if he'd been in a battle or two. My fishing rod looked roughed up as well. Its three-pound test line was stretched even thinner than normal with plenty of nicks; the minnow lure was chewed up, and its hook was bent nearly straight.

Unfortunately, I didn't have a ruler or a scale but my best guess put the tiger musky at 38 inches long and 14 pounds or so. The musky and I posed as a lady in the cheering section snapped a picture of us with her smartphone and emailed me a copy. I now have proof of my catch.

My wife, Kristin, often doubts the accuracy of my fishing stories. I returned the magnificent musky to his home with my heartfelt thanks for the memorable battle. I gave my half-bucket of white bass to other fishermen and wasted no time heading home, excited to tell Kristin yet another of my true-life fishing tales.

#####

INTERCEDE

My dad died before my eyes some years ago. I could not prevent his departure. He wouldn't listen to my entreaties. His perception focused elsewhere as if intent on assisting another. His specter, though, seems unaware of Dad's passing. It is always at the ready to intercede during my times of trouble, whether life threatening or innocuous. Dad's representation is on hand in my imaginings as his person was in my reality. I shall not delve into Dad's countless admirable qualities beyond the scope of this vision as you might believe me to be outside of myself, in a realm of my own creation.

Tonight, I expected Dad's spectral visit. I was returning to my hillside home after wandering the streets during a spectacular evening thunderstorm. Even at my age, I enjoy wading in the roadside rivers, pouncing into the prolific, pothole puddles, the lightning's abstract after images, and the glutted raindrops coalescing into a flowing, silken sheet upon my head.

Dad knocked on my front door as I strode up the driveway. Momentarily illuminated by a lightning flash, he appeared to be aged in his mid-40s, at the height of his business career. Despite the tempest, Dad's signature platinum-blond hair was perfectly kempt in his preferred flat-top fashion. Horn-rimmed glasses upon his pale, Scandinavian visage, darkly outlined, pastel, blue eyes.

Dad's flamboyant, car-dealer's apparel: plaid sports coat, starched, long-sleeve, white shirt with cufflinks, bold tie, contrasting, solid-colored, sharply-creased dress pants, pristine, polished, wing-tipped shoes and his trademark welcoming grin, mirrored my memories.

Dad offered his outstretched hand in greeting and introduced himself as Steve Mitchell. Straightaway, the rains ceased, the rivers completed their journeys, the ponds vaporized, and the lightning's after images cleared.

I was prepared to present to Dad's specter the true nature of its being by way of family photos and documents stored downstairs. As Steve Mitchell and I descended the stairway, we encountered the torrential storm that had ceased outside, a deluge of unfathomable depths, waves, cresting at the ceiling joints. My home was lost.

Dad, a skilled swimmer, dove into the tumult as yet attired in his salesman's panoply. I witnessed his first few underwater strokes. His hair deranged. His glasses were lost. His clothing ruined. His jaw set to an unaffected purpose as he disappeared into the abyss. I agonized in thought, "He can't continue to bail me out of my dread. He can't continue to intercede on my behalf. Why won't he accept his death?"

I screamed, "Where are you? Come back. Let the place flood. This is a nightmare!" I heard the sump-pump circuit breakers being activated.

I yelled, I cried, "I can't bear your death again. Come back, come back! I need you here. Dad, Dad, please!" I could not prevent Dad's selflessness. He would not listen to my pleas. The violence of my emotions woke me suddenly. The flood was gone. My home was saved.

Cora, my wife, made a drowsy-eyed inquiry, "Are you all right?"

Still distraught, I stammered, "Dad, my dad is gone. I, I couldn't stop him. He wouldn't listen to me"

Cora comforted, "It's okay. It's okay. He is safe and so are we."

#####

LAID TO REST

"**M**r. Wehler, is it? I'm your urologist, Dr. Sherman Peebody. Based upon C.T. scans, your kidney mass is most likely a cancer. Even if it is not, we'll still need to remove your kidney in its entirety."

After a 20-minute question-and-answer session, Cora and I agreed to set a surgery date, dependent upon the flow of Dr. Peebody's schedule.

We returned home and had "the talk" in case my life trickles down hill. We covered several subjects, the first of which I'll share.

I explained, "Cora, I'd like my remains to be handled in one of two fashions. You may choose to have me frozen and set aside until your departure. Have the funeral director place me within your coffin, as per normal, in the position of your choice. Please, dear, allow me to finish my inclinations while I'm emotionally stable.

"Secondly, you may choose to have me cremated. When your time has come, have my ashes sprinkled onto your fine frame.

"No matter your preference, we'll be loving each other up for eternity. That's what I call getting 'laid to rest.'"

Cora, in her inimitable fashion, replied, "I'd like to have some time to myself."

#####

CHOCOLATE WIND SONG

The nuclear-stress-test heart specialist, Ian, called me Friday evening, at dinner time, with information, and his list of don'ts for my Monday-morning procedure.

Ian: Mr. Wehler, the test will last two and a half hours.

Mr. Wehler: What? I could give birth in two and a half hours.

Ian: Mr. Wehler, it is mostly waiting for something to happen.

Mr. Wehler: There you go. Please call me Rick.

Ian: Rick, when you arrive, we will inject you with nuclear material and have you rest until it takes effect. Then we will have you lie on the imaging table on your back with your knees up.

Rick: Oh, come on.

Ian: Rick, we will take pictures as a baseline, and then put you on a treadmill and inject more material.

Rick: Alright, Alright, it's Friday. I'm supposed to have fun over the weekend, not be thinking about all of this crap.

Ian: Rick, please do not eat or drink six hours before the test, and do not consume chocolate or caffeinated beverages twelve hours before the test.

Rick: Just a minute. (*I muted the phone.*) Wifey, Sunday night, please feed my remaining malted milk balls, candy bars, chocolate milk and ice cream, and Dr. Pepper to the grandkids. And, and make a note to deduct the restock fees from this geek's bill.

Wifey: Hubber, Sunday night I'm going to spray myself, lightly, strategically, with my own perfume confection, Chocolate Wind Song.

Rick: You're supposed to be on my side. Please pass me the chocolate milk. … Okay, Ian, I'm back.

Ian: Rick, please follow the simple instructions. I do not want you to barf on me.

Rick: Heh, that could be the highlight of my day.

End of the call.

Sunday night, our grandkids pigged out on my post-binge chocolate treats, laughed, talked nonsensically and ran in circles, while I sat on the couch, alone with my thoughts, most of which focused on my chocolate-scented wifey.

Monday morning, Wifey drove us to the appointment, as I was suffering from withdrawal.

Angel, a lighthearted stress-test nurse, greeted us, led me to a treatment room, inserted an IV, and administered ½ milliliter of nuclear material. She said, "You can sit in the waiting room for twenty minutes until the material takes effect."

I replied, "Oh, no! My wife, Cora, is out there, and she smells like chocolate."

Angel looked at me quizzically, smiled politely, and led me to the waiting room.

Twenty minutes later, a sprightly nurse, Ariel, accompanied me to the scanning room. She applied four tapes to my shaggy chest, attached as many electrodes, had me lie flat on my back, raise my hands above my head, and raise my knees off of the table, which she braced with a cushion. She then covered me with a warm blanket.

Ariel encouraged, "Relax. Sleep if you like while the machine takes baseline pictures for thirteen minutes."

Afterwards, she woke and walked me into the nuclear-stress-test lab where I met Ian, who didn't remember who I am.

I made an attempt at witty conversation, "I've been looking forward to this stress test all weekend."

Ian replied, "Mr. Wehler, you have a hairy chest. I must remove these four tapes, shave you, and position ten tapes."

I commented, "Too bad. My wife would enjoy peeling all ten of those off of my hairy chest, slowly."

He went about his business as I thought, "No chest hair, 16 years old again. Okay, Okay, Cora. Twenty-three years old again."

Ian instructed, "Mr. Wehler, we will have you walk on this treadmill that will run one mile per hour for four minutes."

I replied, "We who?"

Ian added, "Here is a chart that lists levels of discomfort once we (I didn't say we who?) inject you with a larger amount of nuclear material. You may feel woozy, light-headed, weak, have blurry vision, abnormal heart beat, and feel the need for a bowel movement."

Ian did a countdown leading to the injection, and after that, a countdown during the injection. As I walked on the treadmill, I felt, "all of the above."

Ian asked, "Mr. Wehler, tell me your discomfort level from this chart."

I tried as best I could to read it, maybe, "Fine, mild, medium, 7, awful, and I gotta take a dump."

I slurred, "Fime."

Ariel returned after my four-minute mile and ushered me to the scanning room once again.

She smiled and stated, "We'll do the same as earlier but for only twelve minutes this time."

Afterwards, she woke me and removed my blanket, knee cushion, the remaining hairless electrode tapes and IV, and escorted me to the waiting room.

Wifey drove us home.

While I slept off the radiation, Cora showered off the Chocolate Wind Song.

#####

MY MYSPACE ACCOUNT
PREFACE

While organizing stacks of stories that I'd written over the past 20 years into alphabetized folders, I came across a few that I'd forgotten and decided to update them. This story is from 2006 when Myspace ruled social networking sites. During that time, I searched my Thesaurus for cool, incomprehensible words to express my thoughts.

It's taken me a while to rewrite this story, as I've had to look up many of the words, figure out what I meant to say, and find an understandable way to say it. I'm beginning to wonder if it's worth Mytime.

###

I relish writing stories early in the day, particularly during the throes of a sugar buzz, sustained by several servings of Lucky Charms cereal. In the recent past, amid a brief, clear-headed episode, I reflected, "It's a shame that I'm my writing's only devotee." I wondered, "How can I form a fan following?"

According to today's wisdom, writers are oftentimes discovered by posting their stories on social networking sites. As a public service, I launched my Myspace account. Although not wishing to post a photo, I did answer a few of the less intrusive questions, such as age and gender. I faked the age and left my gender untouched. I catalogued wisdom beyond my years and a seasoned physique as notable attributes, and humorous writing as a hobby.

That afternoon, I received two correspondences on my Myspace account. The first was an invitation from Miss Tastee Treat:

"Hi Rick,

My name is Tastee Treat. I'm a 19-year-old, natural blond, blue-eyed Norwegian girl who appreciates a man with experience and a spicy body who solicits in writing. I'll be in Sun Prairie this weekend. Would you like to get together for a late-night dinner and a tasty treat?"

The second message was a query from Mr. Bolt Upright, screen name Hayr Trigga, a supposed Wall Street executive of some renown. He wrote:

"Hi Rick,

I enjoy long walks through farm fields and humping peasants with my semi-automatic weapon. (I wondered if he intended to type, hunting pheasants.) Hey Rick, what say we partner up?"

As fulfilling either of these invitations would require actions guaranteed to eclipse my modest sensibilities and dubious dexterity, I exercised my experience and semi-automatic delete key, and terminated my Myspace account.

###

BANTER BATTLES

Cora: Papa, could you please watch little Matteo? I have to go downstairs.
Rick: Okay, as long as he doesn't act like a baby.
Cora: You should talk.

Cora commented, "You've aged, not matured."
I shot back, "That's good news."

As I walked towards the kitchen table carrying a plate, balancing a pecan-caramel roll, Cora said, "Aren't you going to warm it up?"
I put the plate on her lap. She gave me "the look."
I answered, "Hey, hottie. It was your idea."

Cora said, "Shut it! You're 70 years old and five years old at the same time."
I replied, "Am not! Am not!"

We dropped off our Crapsman lawn mower at the repair shop. The rep said, "We'll have it in tip-top form by next week."
Cora asked, "Do you work on husbands?"

Rick: Cora, it's warm. You should wear shorts.
Cora: Nope.
Rick: Hey, you get to enjoy my legs.
Cora: I don't think "enjoy" is the right word.

###

THE WAYS OF LOVE

After 70 years of life and 48 years of marriage, I'm still enrolled in the course, "The Ways of Love." I may not graduate, receive a degree, or throw my cap and tassel into the air. Perhaps the course is its own degree.

I began full-time kindergarten at the age of four. As a result, in high school, I thought of myself as the youngest and smallest person in our class of 436. I didn't date, and considered after-school social activities as an interruption to my work schedule. I yearned for a girlfriend, but I couldn't overcome my insecurity, age, size, and job responsibilities. In hindsight, there were a couple of girls who showed some interest in me, but I wasn't taught the nuances and subtleties of female communication, and was therefore unable to decipher their encrypted messages. The girls took my lack of response as a rebuff rather than inexperience.

At seventeen years old, in the fall of 1967, I undertook classes at the University of Minnesota, Minneapolis campus. College proved to be a culture shock. There were people of all races, nationalities and backgrounds. Ability scored well above confidence, age, stature and employment.

I did well academically during my first quarter. The faculty invited me to enter the honors curriculum, which allowed me to skip the introductory courses to psychology and chemistry, my major and minor. The most notable upgrade was my unexpected entry into "The Ways of Love."

I met my first love during the winter quarter of 1968 in pre-med biology. I was seated at a lab table between two attractive women, Cindy and Phyllis. Cindy, on my left, a small blond who was distraught as her boyfriend was serving in Vietnam. Phyllis, a brunette, was taller than Cindy and equally as beautiful. I was

72

speechless. They both greeted me with kind and gentle voices. I was immediately enamored of them.

Later, after one particularly intriguing lab assignment, dissecting a fetal pig, Phyllis hinted that if we met that evening in the lab, perhaps we could enhance our learning experience. I actually recognized the opening and asked Phyllis to meet me that evening. My very first date: dissecting a fetal pig.

During our forensic encounter, I asked her out to dinner. I did it! I had gotten a date with a smart, kind, and lovely woman, a date that didn't require a face mask and rubber gloves.

I picked up Phyllis at the women's dorm. We drove to a restaurant that I'd frequented with my parents, The Hopkins House. Per my reservation, the hostess seated us at a secluded table for two. I asked her to dim the lights. She did so with a wink and a smile.

Our dinner date was a delightful time of conversation. I worked at being masterful, emulating my father and James Bond, but neither Dad nor 007 could prepare me for the reality of a good-night kiss. Phyllis leaned against the front door to the dorm. I moved in and said, "Goodnight, Cindy." She corrected my blunder, and I departed unkissed.

We met again the next morning at class. She was as sweet as could be and didn't mention my *faux pas.* Later that day, I sent her a dozen jack-o-lantern roses.

During our dinner date, Phyllis had spoken of her dislike for movies and dancing. I had no idea where to go on our next date. She suggested the Minnesota Museum of Art. We shared a wonderful time discussing the paintings and sculptures. We came upon a storeroom crammed with artworks that kept us investigating for the afternoon. I owe her, in part, for my appreciation of art.

On another date, we happened upon a funeral procession. Phyllis began to cry.

I asked quietly, "What's wrong?"

She said, "Haven't you ever had a sympathetic reaction?" She then told me of her marriage engagement that had ended six months earlier.

I comforted, "You're kind and gentle, and a strong woman. You will recover."

Phyllis was tired of supplying dating suggestions, so I relied on my lack of experience and asked her out to the movies. She agreed, reluctantly. We attended *Bonnie and Clyde*, the beginning of my downfall. What a shame, as I was hopelessly in love, and she was perfect in every way.

The following week, I invited her to go dancing at *The Purple Barn*. At the front door, the attendant asked for her I.D. She stated, "I don't have an I.D. I'm 19!" She then took off her coat. The attendant gawked at her figure and immediately admitted both of us. We danced once, a slow dance, with her figure crushed up against me. A good memory, but it turned out that dancing depressed her.

We'd been dating for two months and had not gotten physical. We had an upcoming biology test, and Phyllis suggested that we study at her grandma's apartment. She relegated Grandma to her bedroom, leaving the guest room available. Phyllis had planned to enrich my understanding of the subject. I kept my mind in the books.

The Shrine Circus was in town and my father had an in with a man in the Shriners organization. Dad got us tickets that included a behind the scenes tour. This was going to be the date that made up for all of the others. I picked her up and got hopelessly lost in her presence. Not long thereafter, I was hopelessly lost in downtown Minneapolis. I was so frustrated and angry with myself. I'd lost my way.

Phyllis insisted that I stop the car in a dingy, uninhabited parking lot. She climbed out, walked around in the glow of the headlights, cried, got back into the car and commented, "Maybe we won't have any fun now." I turned the car around, drove back to the dorm, dropped her off, and we never spoke again.

I'm grateful to have gotten another chance at love with my wife Cora. During my tenure in "The Ways of Love," I've learned to recognize her subtle communications but mostly the overt ones, likes, dislikes, expressions of sympathy, and openings for affection, to allow her to love me and me to love her, and myself.

Cora and I have proven that we're meant for each other. I wish, though, that I could've been self-confident while dating Phyllis so that we could both look back at our time together as more than a life experience on which to build, as first loves are precious and never die.

#####

THE WHIZ THAT WAS

"**D**oc, these meds aren't solving my problem."
Dr. Sherman Peebody, my urologist, comforted, "We'll discontinue your current prescription and we'll try a different one."

I replied, "Okay, I'll give it a try."

I picked up the piddle-power pills accompanied by four pages of disclaimers and side effects. The first disclaimer read, "Six to twelve months to begin working. During that time, some of the side effects may become permanent."

The side effects included but were not limited to, my current symptoms and other notables: man boobs, exacerbated prostate cancer, decreased sex drive, and E.D. At the tail end of the listings, "If these occur, discontinue the drug and call your doctor."

I thought, "Yeah, so what's he gonna do, offer an apology and admire my jugs? I have no wish to enhance my figure, my cancer or disappoint my lady."

I explained to Dr. Peebody, bashfully, "Those snow-white pills made me feel grumpy, sleepy, sneezy, and dopey. I'd rather be happy."

Dr. Peebody replied jocularly, "This new prescription should help with your streaming."

Peeved and flushed, I shot back, "All I hope to do is add some power and lessen the time frame to take a whiz. At home, it'd be great if I could take care of business during a TV commercial break without turning on the water faucet. In public, sports fans waiting in line behind me at the urinal have a tendency to get pissed. An outdoor, winter-weather whiz is pointless. I can't even write my initials in the snow."

Pee. S. Wifey commented, "Hubber, this story flows well. You're a whiz at writing."

#####

AFTERTHOUGHTS

"Noah, I'm not looking forward to my next MRI. I don't want to lose any more body parts to cancer."

"Grandpa, you could be like that guy on the Game of Thrones who lost a hand and had it replaced with one made of gold."

"Noah, how do you suppose that works with a prostate?"

Noah and Cora laughed, and Cora made an unkind comment that I couldn't hear.

It's good to have family.

###

"THE LOOK"

R ecently, my heart has been misbehaving. For no apparent reason, at times it races or beats in an irregular fashion. My family doctor referred me to a specialist who recommended a special specialist. I informed my wife, Cora the Dish, "This guy rewires hearts so that 94 percent of the time for rapid heart beat, A-flutter, and 60 percent of the time for irregular heart beat, A-fib, a patient can be healed, but there's no known cure for the heart effects of A-Dish."

Cora gave me, "the look." She invented it to express her dismay soon after my hearing degraded and I began to say, "What?" more often than "Yes, dear." I'd understand "the look" if I was blind, deaf, and dumber.

After a four-month wait for an appointment with the renowned electrophysiologist, Dr. Altar Nate Courent, I ended up spending an hour with his diminutive P.A., (physician's assistant) Ms. Donna Claire "Shortie" Circit. I learned that A-flutter is due to screwed-up nerves on the right side, top of the heart, whereas A-fib is caused by messed-up nerves on the left side top. (I didn't ask about A-Dish.)

Ms. D.C. Circit advised, "You should avoid certain practices that could trigger heart irregularities such as smoking, alcohol and caffeine."

I replied, " I don't partake in any of those."

Cora spoke up, "Add women to the list."

P.A. D.C. smiled and didn't comment.

Dr. A.C. stopped by for six minutes, assured us that my life is not in jeopardy, asked me to sign a form granting him permission to operate, and ordered two tests to be performed before the procedure: a heart MRI and a sleep study.

I inquired, "I had a heart MRI recently, revealing excellent heart health. Why do I need another one?"

He replied, "I want one that focuses on heart rhythm."

I reflected, "No big deal," and then asked, "What is the purpose of the sleep study?"

Dr. Courent answered, "Breathing interruptions while sleeping can cause heart defects."

I thought, "No more bed pillows."

He added, "Most people stop breathing for a few seconds, hourly, and then start back up again."

I acquiesced, "As far as I know, I don't have that problem, but I'll take the test."

It was Tuesday, of course, always my worst day of the week. I had an appointment at the hospital to pick up the sleep-test monitor and take it home overnight. The rep opened the suitcase and described all of the parts that Cora would be strapping onto me. The rep also stated, "You must return the monitor by 11 a.m. Wednesday or they'll assess at $750 charge."

I commented, "That should help my sleep."

Later that evening, Cora sorted through the suitcase's contents and found a folder of forms for me to complete:

1. Description of last night's sleep experience.

I asked the Dish, "I wonder how much detail they require?"

She gave me "the look."

2. A general questionnaire about sleep practices.

"The look" was still in effect, so I said nothing, nothing at all.

3. The morning-after form. Once again, suppressing my impulses, I made no comment. It turned out to be little more than a list of how many times I get out of bed to use the bathroom.

Cora teased, "More than three but less than seven." (My version of "the look," is ineffective.)

Due to my impatience, Cora handled the assembly. She mounted and fastened two straps, one about my chest, the other around my waist, both flaunting electrode connections. She connected the sleep monitor, about the size of three cell phones stacked up, to the chest strap, and then ran wires from the monitor to both the chest and waist straps.

In addition, she snaked two wires from the monitor up opposite sides of my neck, coiled one around each ear, and fixed them onto a cannula in each nostril. I thought, "I'm supposed to sleep hooked up to this contraption?"

Per normal, Cora heard my thoughts and said, "Whine, whine, whine."

I replied, "Wine would help."

Half an hour later, I lay down on my side of Cora's bed and stated, "I'm giving this ten minutes tops." The next thing I remembered was a 3:40 a.m. bathroom visit, and then waking up at 6:30 a.m. I said to myself, because the Dish chose to sleep in another bedroom in case I whined all night, "That's the best night's sleep I've had in a month! Perhaps Medicare will pay for a couple more nights."

We returned the machine on time, no charge, and a week later heard from the sleep clinic, via letter: "You had seven breath interruptions per hour; five is average. The sleep doctor will put in a prescription for a CPAP (continuous positive airway pressure) machine."

I mumbled, and yes, Cora heard me, "This isn't right. The Dish causes at least two of those interruptions per hour, reclaiming her covers."

Cora said, "Whine, whine, whine."

I suggested, "When you get cold in bed, just come on over to my side."

She replied, "That's where all my covers are."

I defended, "A guy's gotta do what a guy's gotta do."

Not soon thereafter, I received a second letter from the sleep clinic that stated, "You will hear from the sleep clinic within ten business days to schedule an appointment to pick up a CPAP machine."

I inquired about a month later, and within a week, received a phone message, informing that I can pick up the CPAP equipment next Tuesday.

We met with the respiratory specialist, listened to the CPAP instructions video, and once again proceeded home with a suitcase. All by myself, I donned the equipment: multifaceted head-straps, attached to a combination nose-and-mouth cover, attached to a four-foot-long, 1.5-inch-diameter elastic hose attached to the machine that I'd set upon my bedside stand.

I mentioned to Cora, "This gizmo will make it difficult to 'make out' but not impossible."

She gave me "the look."

I asked, "What happens if I have to get up to use the bathroom?"

Cora replied, "If? Just disconnect your hose."

I asked shakily, "You mean the machine hose, right?"

She gave me "the look" and said, "Shut it. Just detach the hose right here at the nose-and-mouth mask."

I mumbled, "I'm still uncomfortable about wearing all of this head gear. I'll try it tonight and we'll see how we make out."

Yes, yes, she did.

#####

AFTERTHOUGHTS

Cora is wearing shorts. I couldn't help myself, but I did, and kissed her legs. She gave me "the look."

I said, "Okay, I'm in trouble."

She replied, "Yes! You stopped."

###

QUIPS AND QUOTES

I changed clothes for the festivities beneath a ceiling fan. That was nice because it blew the dust off of my dress shirt.

I stabbed a fork into the pickle jar and got the one I wanted. This is my day!

Cora reads the obits. I don't. We have the same reason: in case I'm in them.

Cora is fully willing to admit when I'm wrong.

Nine-year-old grandson Ethan lectured about forest animals while we were at Westwoods. He told me that many animals are nocturnal while others are diurnal.

I said, "What is diurnal?" He explained and I answered, "You can't know words that I don't." I looked up the word on my phone.

He was correct. I told him that diurnal animals eat nine-year-olds. He explained that he was nine years and four months old and therefore not edible.

###

SEVENTY

Heh, I didn't expect to make it to 57 years old, the age I'd planned to retire. I couldn't imagine reaching 60. Now, I'm one day shy of 70. I'm surprised that my wife, Cora the Dish, has allowed me to live this long. Originally, she had given me until 01-01-2010. After I conquered that point in time, she said, "You've passed your 'use by' date. I'm not going to open that package again." I thought she was teasing.

I mentioned to the Dish, "If I don't make it to 70, please wait at least a year before you remarry."

She replied, "Remarry? No way. I'm looking forward to my independence."

I shot back, "Whaddaya mean? You've been the CEO and CFO of our family ever since I said, 'I do' and 'Yes, dear' in the same breath. I'm just arm candy."

She gave me "the look."

I'm not sure how I'm supposed to feel at 70. As far as I can remember, this is my first go-round. For my entire adult life, which started at 17—or hasn't begun yet, according to Cora—I've been able to handle any challenge except for the Dish.

I've been addicted to weight-lifting since I was a teenager. Last year, my frame mutinied. January 1st, I gave up the obsession and eventually learned that the lack of muscular support rusted my hinges. I took up the habit once again in October, starting at the beginning, as if I were 16. My bod seems to appreciate being ticked-off instead of totally pissed.

My Trek hybrid bicycle is accustomed to traveling far and wide. This past year, it experienced just the opposite.

We bought 65 acres of forested property after my retirement. It's been my hobby to rehabilitate the woodland. After running a chainsaw, hiking with a full backpack, lifting logs, planting trees and confronting unhappy animals for ten years, I'm the one in need of rehab.

I don't remember the number of times my razor-sharp wit has repeated the same joke, or how often I've flipped a non-existent light switch that's positioned on the opposite wall.

On the positive side, I haven't misplaced my glasses or my cell phone this morning.

Last night, I walked past the bathroom mirror and commented "My short-term memory seems to be short-circuiting, but I still look pretty good for my age."

Cora, replied, "You must've forgotten how you look."

This morning, I mentioned to Cora, "I slept well, thanks to your company."

She replied, "Tonight you'll sleep with the fishes."

I hid the bed pillows and the hot-pepper sauce.

Tomorrow, Cora will insist that I wear my DNR/DNI stenciled hat and T-shirt (do not resuscitate, do not intubate) at my birthday party, if I make it to 70.

#####

AFTERTHOUGHTS

Two weeks ago, I decided to put the protective dust cap on my three-year-old sonic toothbrush. Today marks the third day in a row that I've remembered to remove the cap before loading the toothpaste.

I don't want a Facebook avatar. A mirror gives me enough grief.

Back when Cora deflowered this youth, she didn't realize that I'm a perennial.

Cora discarded a can of Code Red Mountain Dew because it lacked effervescence and was beyond its expiration date.

I'M SCARED!

Our son Jerry owns a zero-turn lawnmower manufactured by Gravely. At 70, I don't much care for that brand name.

###

LEFTOVERS

My employer transferred Cora and me to Sun Prairie, Wisconsin, in May of 2000. Due to heredity, which is not my fault, one of my top five orders of business was to find a dentist. With no knowledge of the community, and the lack of Google, I drove down Main Street, bypassed the dentist office with a bank-loan advertisement in the front window, and stopped at the second facility.

Dr. Dennis Chure and I developed a friendship of sorts over the following nineteen years even though he did most of the talking during my office visits. Thanks in part to my frequent patronage, Dr. Den built a state-of-the art dental complex, employing two dentists, many receptionists and hygienists, and an accountant. They all know me by my imperfect smile, missing-molar lisp, and excellent credit rating.

Early on in our relationship, Dr. Den Chure suggested, "We could replace that gummed-up molar with a titanium implant."

I inquired, "How much?"

He replied as if I had this sort of heart attack on a regular basis, "It would cost $4,500 or thereabouts, but at your age, it probably wouldn't pay."

I replied, "For certain 'it' wouldn't pay and neither would I."

I followed up by asking, "How much to pull 'it' out?"

He answered, "$350."

I said, "Do 'it.'"

To my credit, considering my age, I've adapted well to my missing molar's cavern, and Cora has grown accustomed to my speech impediment.

Dr. Den Chure, a few years my junior, has not done well remembering my disfigurement, even though "it" must be in his records. Without fail, at every six-month appointment, he offers, "We could fill that vacancy with a titanium implant."

To which I reply, "No, thanks. That's where I store my leftovers."

#####

AFTERTHOUGHTS

While I dine on a cherry Tootsie Pop, Cora insists that I sit in a room by myself. She doesn't care for the sound of the Tootsie Pop clanking against my teeth. Whereas, I find it comforting to remind me that I still have some.

###

FREAKIN' BOOTS

I mentioned to Cora, "My feet have been a problem recently."
She replied, "They've been a problem for 70 years, but
you've been complaining about them more often lately. It's
time for you to buy new shoes, even though it's not garage sale
season."

I replied, "It's not the Lenten season either. My parents used
to buy me new shoes at Easter for our yearly visit to church."

Cora is familiar with one of the few full-service shoe stores
remaining in Wisconsin. We traveled for 55 minutes through city
traffic. She drove. I rode shotgun with my eyes closed.

The representative at Foot Freaks Shoes 'n Such, Clete
Sandall, introduced himself with a soft European accent and a
handshake to match. I noticed that he was wearing namesake
footwear and pedicured toes...in February. Cora identified the
sandals as a foreign, designer label that she'd love to own, but
they're too pricey.

Clete insisted on removing my shoes and measuring my
stocking-footed feet with a tool that I hadn't seen in use since my
teen years, which was the last time I'd bought shoes from a shoe
store.

I mentioned, "My size-13 feet need support and laces that tie
above the ankles."

Sandall tripped to the backroom and returned five minutes
later burdened by six shoe boxes. He removed a pair of mid-height
hiking boots from box number three, installed orthotic, arch-
support inserts from box five, and slid one team onto each of my
feet.

He secured the boots in a peculiar fashion, by wrapping the
boot strings upwards around the lower boot-lace hooks and

wrapping downwards on the top set of hooks, before he tied them off. I thought, "What a salesman."

The boots felt fine after a nine-step test walk. Clete then removed the boots and replaced them with black tennis shoes from box number two, enriched by the same inserts. They felt capable as well during the test walk.

Cora commented, "They don't lace above his ankles."

Sandall bent my old tennies in half showing how they were no longer rigid and offered no support. He then challenged Cora, "Try and bend these Foot Freaks shoes."

I thought, "Mistake!"

After working through the remaining boxes and another four that he'd procured, Cora and I settled upon three likely candidates for purchase. Clete had not mentioned prices as I admired the shoes, and he my feet.

Before I popped the question, Cora mentioned to Sandall, "Rick wears slippers when he's at home." He excused himself with a slight bow, and returned shortly thereafter with a set of slippers. They boasted open-toe display (not a good idea), built-in arch supports of soft German wood, German leather, and two Velcro straps, most likely German. They were comfy and he didn't ask Cora to bend them.

I asked, "What's the price of the boots, the tennis shoes, the orthotic inserts, and the slippers?"

Clete Sandall replied, having lost his accent, (my thoughts are in parenthesis) "$265 for the (freakin') boots, $165 for the (you've got to be kidding me) tennis shoes, $75 for the (lame-ass) orthotic, arch-support inserts—and wait for it—$365 for the (#&*>ing) slippers."

The prices rattled me. I wondered, "Who, in their right mind, would pay $365 for a pair of #&*>ing slippers?"

I commented, "What's the total? I don't have a calculator."

Clete replied as he opened his phone, "No problem."

I advised, "Forget the (#&*>ing) slippers."

He answered, "$505...plus tax."

I looked at Cora and muttered, "That's more money, adjusted for inflation, than I've spent or will spend on footwear in my entire existence, including the three past lives that I'm aware of and the one to come."

Cora said, "It's time for us to spend some money on ourselves. Let's buy good stuff instead of garage-sale bargains."

I replied, "I'm not sure that I've enough time remaining in my lives to make them pay."

We agreed to purchase the boots and the arch supports, and on the way home, stop for a hot-fudge milkshake at our local Culver's.

Clete Sandall stated, "That will be $340 plus tax."

He then suggested that we purchase a $3 can of waterproof spray for $12 even though the boots are waterproof.

When we arrived home. I set our purchases aside, not willing to wear them until I'd calmed down.

I awoke at 3 a.m. the next morning in a cold sweat. I mumbled, "How could I have been such a dumbass to spend that much money on inserts and shoes? Not even shoes. They're freakin' boots. My life's training of frugality, all shot to hell at Foot Freaks."

Cora woke up, thanks to my discourse, and I explained the reason for my wet pajamas.

She comforted, "We have seven days to return them for a full refund."

I thanked her and replied, "I'm going to wear these freakin' boots, with their lame-ass inserts, every waking moment for six days. On the seventh day, after their return, I shall rest."

#####

AFTERTHOUGHTS

Cora ordered, "Trim your toenails before you wear sandals."

I replied, "No need. I'll wear socks too. Would black or brown be better?"

WANNABE

While working in the Westwoods forest, I stole away to take care of some pressing personal business. Thereafter, I hiked up my jeans and went back to my project. I felt something crawling in my private places, shook my pants, and felt the intruder descend to the back of my knee.

I've often been stung while involved in forestry projects without much concern but I swear this bugger vaccinated me with a flu-shot syringe. I screamed a litany of religious names and impolite expressions that shook the pious pines, smacked my left knee pit, and dropped trou. A 1950's horror movie wannabee, the size of a turkey vulture, fell to the ground. It left behind an impressive puncture that mushroomed before my eyes.

I reflected, "That beetch is dead and I'm not. Two minutes ago, it could've been a real pisser."

#####

BANTER BATTLES

Cora looked at the container of Bloom Grow in the garden center.

I asked, "Are you going to sprinkle that on me?"

Grandson Noah commented, "That's Bloom Grow, not weed killer."

###

"Cora, I had to tighten up my hat."

"Rick, you're losing gray hair and gray matter."

###

"Cora, I'm going to start taking fish oil pills. They're supposed to be good for brain function."

"Hubber, you should have started thirty years ago."

###

Cora walked in as I was making the bed and said, "The bed skirt is too short."

I replied, "It'd look great on you."

Cora left the room as Rick was making the bed.

###

I commented, "It's leap-year day. It's customary for women to propose."

Cora replied, "Maybe next time."

###

"Wifey, if you had an identical twin, I would've married both of you."

"Hubber, no! Not even if we were conjoined."

###

BUYOUT

When I retired in 2007, I set my wife, Cora, as the beneficiary of my pension if something were to happen to me. As a result, the company reduced my monthly payout based upon the most recent studies that show women live 2.5 years longer than men. Today, 12 years later, my heredity predicts that I'm five years overdue, whereas Cora's family is just shy of immortal. Her mother, Ma Johnson, made it to 89, Aunt Lila is 95, and Uncle Roger is 102!

Recently, I received a mailing from an accounting firm representing the company that bought the company that bought the company that bought my employer, offering me a buyout of my monthly retirement payments. The stuffed-to-the-suffering-point envelope contained enough printed-on-one-side papers to replace a mega roll of Charmin tissue, although less applicable. All with the purpose of burying me in a bumload of legalize and confounding figures.

I'm a former grocery store produce man, experienced in the arts of displaying and selling fruits and vegetables. No doubt this company has a cadre of actuaries, each with his or her own cubicle and laptop, any one of whom surpasses my 1040 standard deduction, accounting skills by powers of ten.

In brief, I'm offered: a buyout in cash or rolled over into an IRA, an increased pension with reduced benefits to Cora in the event of my demise, or just leave things as they are. There, I said it all in one sentence, not 35 freaking pages.

With a big-numbered, senior-citizen calculator in hand, I figured that the lump-sum buyout offer equals 14.19 years of my pension. According to publications by the Social Security System, Cora's life expectancy, at her age, is an additional 20 years (plus her unaccounted hereditary enhancement). I'm no actuary but 20 minus 14.19 is about six years shy of reasonable.

After flipping through the stack of legalize and figures, I slid it into the shredder and decided to continue my monthly pension payments as they were.

Cora was sitting at the kitchen table, working through the newspaper's crossword puzzle, which is her normal, early-morning practice. I shared with her the buyout options offered by the accounting firm and my astute recommendation. She nodded politely, entered neandertal into the crossword puzzle and consented to my decision.

I added, "There's one caveat."

She replied, "Okay?"

I insisted, "You must promise to live at least another 14.19 years!"

She replied, "How are you going to know?"

#####

YOU MIGHT BE A VEGMAN IF ...

For years I was the regional director of produce and floral operations for a midwestern grocery store chain. During that time, I sent letters weekly to the company director, store directors, and produce managers, detailing market conditions, upcoming promotions and display recommendations.

Somewhere along the line, I took on the moniker, The Vegman. I set up my license plate with that nickname and signed all of the letters accordingly. I borrowed the signature line of Jeff Foxworthy, "You might be a redneck if," and altered it to read, "You might be a Vegman if ..." I added the altered, signature line, followed by a punchline, as a PS to the letters. I had hoped to lighten up the tense business atmosphere with a little produce humor. Below is a sampling.

You might be a Vegman if ...

- Wifey is hot for your celery-scented bod.
- You've been reprimanded for being late to work at 4:05 a.m.
- A Mac is an apple not a computer.
- Jergens Lotion doesn't soften your hands.
- You've slipped on produce and fallen so often that you could teach a course in proper technique.
- A story goes along with every box-cutter scar.
- Your kid, just out of college, makes double your wage.
- Your body clock doesn't understand vacations.
- You've had a pallet of produce parked on your foot.
- The backroom pinup poster is a color chart for bananas.

- Wifey doesn't question the red stains on your collar during the strawberry season.

- The dryer's lint screen is clogged with twist ties.

- You've never seen a tarantula in a box of bananas.

- Today's gut ache relates to the shipment of new-season cherries.

- You can throw a cherry tomato around a corner.

- Fruit basket orders always arrive ten minutes before quitting time.

- You're the only one who knows about cardone and burro bananas.

- You're told that you have bad pits. Your first thought is to check the soft fruit display.

- You get upset when customers mess up your displays.

- Strip rotate is not as interesting as it sounds.

- Your tie-died work shirt didn't start out that way.

- After a long workday, your hands aren't allowed near the wife.

- Leek soup and anise candy don't sound gross.

You might be a Vegman if …

- Washing your apron produces soup stock.

- You laughed while watching a customer try to weigh a watermelon on a hanging scale.

- T&A is a vegetable grower not a female, body-parts reference.

- You remember when grapes came in only two colors, green and red.

- A Golden Delicious is an apple not a hot blond.

- You go to bed before your kids.

- The boss always calls just as you settle down in the john.
- You celebrate major holidays because you survived.
- The cooler used to be your break room and smoking lounge.
- Your neighbors shopped at your store.
- You've gone "postal" with a fruit or a veggie.
- The cherimoya you couldn't sell is splattered on the cooler wall.
- Your pants have holes in the pockets due to ink pens and box cutters.
- Fruit flies help you locate the spoiled tomato on the display.
- Your fingers have more furrows, gouges and potholes than the road in front of Uncle Bud's house trailer.
- You'd rather have the boss shop your department than the wife.
- Most of your coffee break is spent answering the phone.
- You have more bosses than employees.
- A sparrow flies around in your department.
- You've unloaded a watermelon delivery one at a time over the side of a semi-trailer truck.
- You've never met a watermelon truck driver with all of his front teeth intact,
- A vacation is two days off in a row.
- You remember when bananas were overpriced at 19 cents a pound.
- The demo girls were babes not seniors connected to oxygen tanks.

You might be a Vegman if ...

- Twist ties make great toothpicks.

- You hired on as a Vegman when the job was sought after due to high wages and abundant overtime.

- You get blamed for B.O. after culling the rotten potatoes.

- You shared the backroom with the store furnace, the maintenance slop sink and the pop-bottle storage area.

- Your first produce manager spoke mostly in four-letter words.

- Your solid-color work shirts are now psychedelic.

- You displayed watermelon outside in 90-degree heat and hosed them down daily to get rid of the sticky stuff, clean the sidewalk, and limit the fly population.

- An overheated watermelon exploded in your face.

- It took two seasons to convince customers that nectarines aren't bald peaches.

- Even you're not sure about a plumcot.

- You carry extra newspaper coupons in your shirt pocket.

- You can smell mold in a box of citrus before you open it.

- There's nothing like building a cool display to make you feel like your day has been worthwhile.

- You've made rude comments comparing produce items to body parts.

- While cleaning the produce tables, you found a name badge, an ink pen and thirty-six cents in change.

- Your wife feels that you can't adapt to change even though you do so on a daily basis, but for safety's sake, she's right.

- A produce manager meeting is a day away from the store and free food.

- You choked the backroom garbage disposal with bad peaches, and laughed as it spattered peach-pit bullets.

- Fame for a great sales week lasts for a day. Blame for a bad sales week lasts until the next great one.

- Your vegetable misters spray the mirrors, chrome, customers and at times the vegetables.

- The customer's special order is on the late truck, located in the nose of the trailer, on the bottom of a sideways pallet.

- Your t-shirts and ball caps have produce logos.

- You've learned to wash your hands before handling something personal.

- You're always in season!

Vegmen, it's 4pm. You've put in your twelve-hour shift, trimmed the celery, culled the potatoes, filled the displays, wrecked your clothes, roughed up your hands, and slipped on a grape. Buy a bouquet, head home and romance the wife.

#####

The Whims of Nature

D ad was in control of life as we knew it. He chose the design of our home and had it built at the furthest reaches of the rutted, dirt paths that encircled Lake Charlotte, a swamp in the midst of new housing development. Within two years, the paths had been transformed into paved roads with such names as Norwood Drive, Elm Drive and Birch Road, and many homes had joined us.

He created a beautiful yard with an impeccable lawn, young trees and planter boxes packed with flowering shrubs. At Dad's direction, my sisters, Ru and Bun, and I were the caretakers. As we soon learned, even Dad was subject to the whims of nature in southern Minnesota.

May 6th, 1965, Dad was home for supper, an unusual occurrence. As a car salesman, he didn't get paid unless he was on hand at the dealership romancing customers. As the skies darkened well before sunset, Dad, Mom, Ru, Bun, and I walked outside into the front yard to see what was going on. Thick gray clouds had filled the sky, and the wind howled as it crossed the swamp and whipped Dad's new trees.

Suddenly, it got quiet and the clouds began to rotate above us. Dad ordered, "Girls, head to the basement." He turned to me and said, "Rick, we're going to check on the big trees in the backyard."

As we arrived, I heard a fump and spotted what looked like a softball punched into the sod. Curious, I ran over and picked up a conglomerate of hail stones bigger than my fist. Just then, another struck behind me. Dad yelled, "Get back here now!"

I retreated with Dad beneath our roof overhang. The sky cut loose with giant hailstones for less than a minute, but long enough to cover our backyard. After the pelting stopped, we gathered a few of the biggest hailstones to show the girls, smiled at each other and stared into the dark gray clouds, wondering if more hailstones would fall.

The churning clouds sunk closer to the ground and swept over the tall trees that lined the border of our backyard. We hiked to a hilltop behind our yard and watched as the storm sped across the fields. Minutes later, the rotating clouds touched down on the horizon. The funnel grew huge and black as it gathered debris that circled around it.

Dad said, "We're heading to the basement. There could be another one coming."

We learned the next morning that the tornado, an F4, had ripped through Chanhassen, a neighboring town. Several others had touched down in communities surrounding Lake Minnetonka, a magnificent lake not far away, and had done untold damage.

Dad said, "Rick, we're heading out on the boat."

We drove to Lake Minnetonka where Dad docked his Chris Craft, inboard speed boat. It was unharmed. We boarded and motored slowly out onto the calm waters. Within minutes, we came across an overturned boat with a two by four sticking through its hull. Continuing on, we spotted other boats in similar condition, and trees that had been ripped up and thrown into the lake.

Dad turned towards a bay that sheltered a popular marina. The boats were thrown helter-skelter. He weaved between them moving closer to the marina. The tornado had destroyed the buildings, boats and docks, and piled the debris into a junkyard heap taller than our house.

Dad said, "We're going home before we get in trouble with the authorities."

The following winter, a snowstorm moved in overnight and buried our young neighborhood. Dad had to make it to work. I wondered, "How many people want to buy a car in this weather?"

Dad ordered, "Rick, suit up. We're taking Mom's VW Beetle out for a drive. It'll have better traction than the Fairlane." As I watched, Dad hit the gas, backed that 40-horsepower football helmet out of the garage and plowed it onto Birch Road where the snow topped its fenders.

Dad shouted, "Stand on the back bumper and grab onto the side window ledges. You're extra traction."

We took off down Birch Road, weaving whichever way the snow tugged and Dad countered. The snow flew around me and coated my eyeglasses, but I could see around the edges.

Dad had explained, "When we make it to Excelsior Boulevard (the main road), I'll drop you off, head to work, and you can hike home."

We made it a quarter-mile to the base of the hill that is Seymour Drive before we got bogged down. Dad's best efforts couldn't get us ten feet further. He dropped the driver-side window and yelled, "Get off. I'm going to swing this buggy around." Dad hit the gas on Mom's snow cone and veered into the path that we had made on the way out." Dad hollered, "Get in. We've got a trail so I won't need extra traction."

As I opened the passenger door, a husky dog appeared out of nowhere, ran up to our car, jumped through the open door ahead of me, and curled up on the backseat.

The three of us skied home without a problem. As we slid into the garage, Dad ordered, "Break out your snow shovel."

I don't remember what happened to the husky. I do remember spending a good share of the rest of my life shoveling our sidewalk and driveway.

#####

QUIPS AND QUOTES

In seventh grade, my shop teacher, Mr. Johnson used to say, "Careful on the band saw Wehler or your fingers will be even all the way across." I heard something similar when Cora and I were dating and I tried to cop a feel. The same thing happened last night and this morning.

I understand that I'm not even close to being right all the time. I don't know how wives do it!

Cora is gone for the week. The entire bed is mine, but I'm gonna sleep in the guest rooms three nights out of four just as if she's home.

I just learned that the pajama pants Cora bought me are made out of material that wicks away moisture.

Hallmark movies, nobody swears, no guns or explosions, perfect hair and everybody keeps their clothes on. Unrealistic. Total waste of TV time!

A friend at the grocery store changed jobs.
I asked, "You got promoted?"
He replied, "No, I'm an underling."
I encouraged him, "Wait 'till you get married."

Our neighbor has set up a deer-hunting, ground blind at Westwoods for the upcoming season. In the meantime, I've found it to be a cozy outhouse.

EARLY RISER

For years, I've owned a dependable, electric alarm clock with a red number display, dubbed Early Riser, Early for short. It's a simple model, without a radio, just numbers that blink when the minutes or hours change.

When I need to get out of bed before I wish for my part-time retirement job, I set the alarm and then wake up a dozen times or so overnight to read the display.

Recently, my work schedule changed. As I tried to reset the alarm by depressing the alarm button while also depressing the hour button and then the minute button, the minute button declined to advance the display.

No amount of friendly persuasion could convince Early to allow me an additional thirty minutes of clock-watching before I arise.

Unwilling to give up my bedtime companion, I get up thirty minutes earlier than I wish. Thanks to the extra time, I need not lay out my clothing, the breakfast dishes and cereal the night before. Unfortunately, my OCD will not allow such a lifestyle change.

Therefore, today, I lay on the edge of our bed without my eyeglasses and stared at Early Riser through thirty blinking minute changes, and unplugged him. No more Early reminders to start the day. I cleaned his blank display screen with Windex, laid him, along with his ever-present cord, in a small, plastic WetWipes box, clicked it shut, said a few thoughtful words, and pitched him into the recycle bin.

I recruited the electric alarm clock from our guest bedroom, an area occupied solely by me on nights when my company in our bedroom is not appreciated. Said clock has red numbers that are dim, fuzzy and nearly illegible. I traded the crippled clock for the model in our second guest bedroom, which, at times, I occupy as a change of pace.

The second guest bedroom clock exhibited the same faults.

There must have been an electrical malfunction caused by the nearby lightning strike that voiced such a thunderclap that I awoke, without an alarm clock, but with the need for an immediate bathroom visit. When I exited the facility, adorned in different jammies, I found every electric clock in the house blinking 12:00.

Later that day, Cora purchased her guest-rooms hermit a new, red-numbered alarm clock. It boasts a steady display that stands two inches tall, illumination that far exceeds that of Early, and the former guest-room clocks, which also rest in the recycle bin, and a night light in case I need to find the bathroom in a hurry.

I can read Early Riser II's time without my glasses and with my eyes closed, if I'm sleeping in our bedroom.

#####

WITHIN A WEEK OR SO

L ast night, before bed, while donning my jammies, I draped my summertime wear—t-shirt, shorts, socks, and lack of underwear—over the side of our jacuzzi tub.

This morning, as I dressed in preparation for a bike ride, I couldn't find my wallet. It's proven to be a good practice to have I.D. on board due to my disregard for country road traffic and stop signs. I had my wallet yesterday when I stopped by an estate sale and spent $2 on a jug of assorted bouncy balls for our grandkids. Is it possible that someone picked my pocket? If so, the laugh's on them. My anorexic wallet is thinner than a dollar-menu burger.

For reasons that escape me, I began the search-and-rescue mission in our garage by dumping out the trash can and the recycle bin onto the garage floor. As I dug through the crap, I proposed to do a better job of sorting recyclables, refilled the can and the bin, swept the entire garage, and rearranged some of the wall hangings.

I then rifled through our SUV, cleaned beneath the seats, vacuumed the floor mats, arranged the glove compartment, and found 73 cents but no wallet.

Somewhat concerned, I concentrated on our living room furniture, dislodged every couch and chair cushion, found a broken rubber band, a comb, and a cat's eye marble but no wallet. As long as the cushions lay helter-skelter upon the floor; I jumped from one to the other, pretending that the carpet was hot lava. Before replacing the mostly undamaged cushions and wrapping my sprained ankle, I vacuumed the furniture's insides.

I looked beneath anything that has an underneath, including but not limited to the beds and the kitchen appliances. The beds sheltered several colonies of dust bunnies and scads of Cora's purses but no wallet. I put the vacuum to use once again, emptied it twice, and gently replaced Wifey's abandoned purses.

The walls behind the dislodged, wallet-free kitchen appliances appeared dingy. Their potty-water hue is now a zesty blue-gray.

I opened the door to Cora's girl cave/office, quickly closed it, and spent the day hoping that she'd not discover my intrusion.

Yes! My downstairs gym where I exercise, stretch and generally piss off uncooperative muscles and joints. Perhaps I set my wallet on the table alongside the achievement charts. No, nothing there but a snowballing pile of shredded paper.

Yes! My man cave/furnace room. Nope.

Okay, I'm freaked out! I tried calling Cora, who is currently in northern Michigan taste-testing Aunt Judy's collection of high-end wines. Apparently, cell phone communications are not a priority in Lake Leelanau. Eventually, we connected as she stood on a chair in Aunt Judy's back bedroom. Cora didn't calm me down, but did offer instructions on how to contact the credit card company, AAA and the police department.

The folks at Card Member services cancelled my Visa card immediately and promised to mail me a new one, within a week or so.

AAA emailed me a paper copy to fill in until a replacement card arrives, within a week or so.

With permission, I borrowed $25 from Cora's no-longer-secret cash stash, and drove, driver's-license-free, to the police station. The front desk clerk suggested that I proceed to the DMV on Battalion Road in Madison.

"WaWTF (Where and WTF) is that?" I didn't say it, just thought it.

Upon arrival, at the DMV, Department of Motor Vehicles, thanks to Google Maps, I found an auditorium packed from wall to wall with rows of chairs filled with people of all impatient ethnicities, religions, ages, and genders.

The lady at the information desk handed me a form to fill out and directed me to the "photographer." The computer-camera person sucking on a Tootsie Roll Pop, flicked my pic (mugshot) and handed me a slip of paper imprinted with the number C201. I asked, "Do you have a pen that I could borrow to fill out this form?"

She replied, "They're over on one of the counters. You'll have plenty of time to find one and fill out the form. They're currently serving L561."

"WaWTF!" I didn't say it.

I found an empty chair kitty-corner from an obese, elderly lady with a three-pronged, spear-tipped cane, and a "don't mess with me" stare. Not long thereafter, a hulking guy, wearing tat sleeves and a yellow, wife-beater t-shirt emblazoned with, "Eat More Muffins," took possession of a recently vacated chair across from me, and fidgeted relentlessly.

In the course of time, a computer voice called my number and I wove my way through the congregation to counter #4. Fourteen dollars later, I had a temporary, paper driver's license and an assurance that my duplicate license would arrive within a week or so.

Google Maps directed me home via fewer streets and wrong turns than I would normally curse.

I had a piece of last week's chicken for dinner, followed by a generous helping of caramel-crunch ice cream, avoided the national news on TV, and decided to mellow out in our deactivated jacuzzi. We had shut down the jets years ago after experiencing their proficiency at assaulting unprotected body parts.

As I leaned over the edge of the tub to wipe up the debris from my last occupancy, there sat my wallet, snagged on a useless arm rest. I latched on to the escapee, verified that my remaining allowance, $23, was unspent, and shredded the cards, hoping that all will be replaced within my lifetime.

#####

MY BET

I commented to Cora, "I'm nervous about this appointment with the heart specialist."

Cora comforted, "We'll be fine."

I replied. "You've always been and will always be *FINE*, little wifey. I, on the other hand…"

September 27th, 2019, the heart surgeon explained the ablation procedure to us in a simple, direct fashion that I did not want to understand. Dr. Altar Nate Courent stated, "In order to stabilize your heart rhythm, our team will enter your heart with IVs through two groin veins, one on each side of your abdomen. While in your heart, we'll poke a hole through the wall between the top two chambers and cauterize the offending nerves in the left chamber. Then we'll retreat and do the same in the right chamber. Essentially, we're rewiring your heart. You'll recover quickly."

I looked over to Cora and said, "You rewired my heart when we met fifty years ago. I still haven't recovered."

A month later, Dr. Courent's assistant, Ms. Val Hart called and we set up an appointment for 1-29-2020. I mentioned to Cora, "I have three months to live. I'm going to prepare a list of projects that I must complete before I'm toast."

Cora said, "Don't think that way. It's my bet that you'll come through it and recover well."

I replied, "Maybe so but that's not my bet. I'm going to be sure we're ready.'

My projects included:

- Update our financial accounts. Those that I'm aware of.

- Arrange a fun family get together before my surgery.

- Review my stories and books so that when I'm dead, rich and famous, our family can cash in.

- List who inherits what of my belongings. Those that remain after Cora's latest garage sale.

- Prepare our 2019 taxes.

- Get all the loving my heart can handle. Cora...Cora, where are you?

###

On surgery day, we got up at 5 a.m. for the 6:30 a.m. appointment. I dressed in whatever I could find in my daze.

We arrived on time and signed in. A nurse escorted us to my private, one-bed closet, and instructed me to undress and put on a backside-challenged gown. Cora watched in awe.

A different nurse arrived and installed an IV into my right arm, followed by a nurse who installed a portal into my left arm. Several residents, surgical nurses and two anesthesiologists stopped by, introduced themselves, asked the same questions, and made sure I didn't have any loose teeth.

A young, attractive nurse's aide stepped into my closet with a battery-powered shaver. Within minutes, I was bald from my neckline to even with my equipment. Cora commented, "A manscape. I could've done that for you at home, slowly, with a tweezer."

I replied, "Yeah. A shame I missed out on that."

She continued, "That's going to itch. You'll have to figure out how to scratch politely."

I said, "I suppose you'll want to help, impolitely."

I laid back on the bed as instructed, and yet another nurse wheeled me into the operating room while my gown wafted flirtatiously in the breeze. One of the gowned surgical staff—not my type of gown—pressed a clear, rubbery mask onto my face and ordered me to breathe deeply. A talkative nurse, not addressing me, removed what remained of my apparel, lifted my torso off the bed, twisted me sideways, and pasted big patches onto my hairless back and chest. Someone disagreed with the arrangement.

Together they jostled me about, tore off the patches, repositioned them, felt better of it, and repeated the process.

I heard someone say, "You're going to feel sleep…

I awoke two minutes later as the aerobics continued. The wall clock had warped four and half hours into the future. I mumbled, "Is that clock a joke? I'm going to be pissed if I'm aboard a spaceship and aliens have been pasting and removing patches all this time."

One of the crew smiled and beamed me into the recovery room.

Four hours later, I found myself drifting from the recovery room into a private cabinet in the cardiac wing.

Cora was there. I commented, "Your face is the first one I wanted to see if I lived, not those patch-pasting Klingons."

She asked, "Patch-pasting Klingons?"

We visited for a while. I'm a bit foggy about what, probably my extraterrestrial experience and my manscape.

A nurse stopped by and yanked out my urinary catheter in a nanosecond.

I shouted, "Yikes."

She reacted, "Fast is less painful than slow."

As she left the room, I muttered, "In that case, I'm glad Cora didn't remove it."

Cora requested, "Hubber, I'd like to stay overnight."

I suggested, "Why don't you go home and get some rest. I won't lack attention."

She replied, "Okay. I'm sure Dr. Leonard McCoy is on your planet."

I was right about the attention. A nurse stopped by every three hours to wake me up, ask if I had trouble sleeping, take my blood pressure, and check on all of my bandaged punctures.

When Cora arrived the next morning, she asked, "How're you feeling?"

I replied, "My chest is okay, but my throat's sore. I can barely swallow."

Cora activated her phone flashlight and commanded, "Open wide and say aaaahhhh."

I said, "Aaaahhh, baby."

That got me "the look" so I complied.

She yelled, "Oh, my gosh," took a picture, left the room and returned shortly with a nurse who followed the same procedure, including the phone picture and the comment. Soon a threesome of physician assistants stopped by, did the same, as did a cardiac surgeon.

Cora handed me her phone and said, "Look at this picture."

I replied, "No, thanks. I'm living it and don't want to see it."

Cora informed, "It turns out that the anesthesiologist damaged your uvula."

I replied, "What? Isn't that a female body part?"

I got "the look" again and an explanation.

I commented, "That guy must've damaged my throat when he shoved the exhaust-pipe intubation hose down my face."

One of the photographers posted the pictures of my damaged, masculine uvula on the hospital computer system, and Mr. Intubate had some explaining to do. He stopped by, mumbled a bit, and offered a meek handshake. I didn't want to be a dick, so I shook his hand.

A nurse stopped by to help me get dressed. She tried to limit the view, but that's a lost cause with a hospital gown and an unbalanced (physically) patient. As Cora held me up by my left arm and nurse by my right, I made an effort to step into my pants. I commented, "Left leg in, check. Legs two and three, check." Cora and the nurse laughed. I looked at them quizzically and said, "What?"

We left for home around noon.

Two days later, when I summoned up the courage, Cora carefully changed all of my bandages. She said, "Those bruises are impressive, but they'll pale in comparison to the ones I'll provide if you don't continue to do what I tell you to do."

I mumbled, "Yes, dear."

That evening, I commented to both Cora and our grandson Noah. "I didn't expect to be alive. I lost my bet."

Noah comforted, "That's okay, Grandpa. So did I."

Cora chimed in, "Just my luck. I won. Oh, well. Pay up you two."

AFTERTHOUGHTS

It's been a good day. I woke up...twice.

Tomorrow, if the surgeon says that I can stop taking pills, then I won't forget to take them as often.

I got dressed and put on deodorant for my follow-up phone call appointment with the heart surgeon. It went well. I'm down to one pill per day, and it isn't blue.

###

BANTER BATTLES

Cora threw her shoulders back and said, "Do you want to play with the girls?"

I answered enthusiastically, "Yessss!"

She gave me "the look" and said, " I meant that your little granddaughters are coming over."

I replied, "That's not the way I heard it."

Cora told Noah, "Grandpa and I went garage saling and bought a baby-bouncy seat, not for Grandpa the big baby."

Noah replied, "That's good because babies are supposed to be cute."

Cora asked, "May I read your texts with Noah's mom?"

I replied, "Sure, you can read all of my texts except those with Jennifer Lopez."

Cora added, "That's fair, if you don't read my texts with Shemar Moore and A-Rod."

Noah commented, "The only texts Grandpa would receive from J-Lo are cease-and-desist orders."

Cora said, "I added $20 to your wallet. You now have $47 and can afford to buy me dinner."

I replied, "Great. Pizza Hut has a special on large, two-topping pizzas at $7.99, and they deliver."

I complained, "Noah, Grandma will be gone Tuesday through Friday, maybe even Saturday next week. It's just you and me."

Noah replied, "Yeah? Looks like I'll be babysitting."

BOOK II

FEMAILS

Left to right: Ru, Bun and Rick.

ALIENS
(9-21-1998)

Hi Bruder,

I just got a voicemail from my writing critic. I've been forwarding some of your emails to him because they're hysterical. He said, "Your brother obviously has the same writing talent as you. You should encourage him to submit some comedic writing somewhere. His stuff is hysterical."

So there you have it. He's a prolific reader who has given me my best suggestions and criticisms, so take it seriously.

My rebuilt hand isn't throbbing today. PTL. So, I celebrated by oinking-out at the Olive Garden where I took my glove off and didn't scare any little kids. I'm stuffed and disappointed. So what's new with you?

Dear Robobabe/Cybersis,

Always good to hear from my technologically advanced, alien baby sister.

You and your critic are correct. I do write hysterically. Please let him know that Wifey has submitted several examples to a prestigious asylum.

I've been depressed the past few days. Tonight, in your honor, I'm cheering myself up by watching the sci-fi movie Aliens on HBO. I went to see it in the theater when it first came out. I brought along three changes of underwear, a box of Depends, and a chamber pot. I ran out of supplies ten minutes before the closing credits. Now that I'm older and realize that Aliens is most likely science fiction, all I need while laying on the living room carpet watching the show is a rubber sheet.

These creatures were created under my bed when I was a child. Cora the Dish, my wifely bedmate, her bowie knife and the

1911A, Colt 45, Combat Commander with its extra-long, 15-shot clip, and Eagle Claw hollow-point ammo that rest in her nightstand, guarantees that aliens wouldn't dare to exist under our bed. Even so, I'm sleeping on the couch tonight.

I'm sure that Cora will be safe. She's known throughout my universe as "Coran the Dishtroyer." If I'm wrong and such aliens do exist beneath our bed, then tomorrow morning I'll enter our bedroom, lay out my rubber sheet, wrap up, and remove their dismembered bodies.

Okay, I'm back.

On the way home today, I had a medium-sized mind-blaster known as a DQ chocolate malt. I don't know why people spend millions on drugs when for $2.10 including tax, they can purchase two hours worth of pure psychedelia.

Morgan Fairchild, a man for a first name and a blond kid for a last name.

Whenever I type words like name, where the n is before the m, for some reason, I switch the letters, and I have to retype the word. It's probably something Freudian, like I'm thinking of our mother.

Son Andy is doing fine. Thanks for not asking. I bought a five-pound box of Spanish Clementines. (Ha, the m is first in this word.) Andy ate eight of them. Actually seven, but I like the sound of "ate eight." They're seedless tangerines. I don't eat them because I always chomp down on a seed. Soon, Andy will be looking for the Depends and the rubber sheet. After 21 years of his adolescence, revenge is sweet.

Toby is OK. Thanks for not asking. He's been going to a lot of parties lately. Then he comes home.

Jerry is fine. Thanks … mevernind. He says little about his days pro or con. Oops, I'm not supposed to use the word "con" when speaking of Jerry.

Mother sent me four boxes of her homemade candy. I'm sure that it's swimming in sugar. The first peice was peanut butter chunk. (Shut the hell up, spell checker. I know the rule: i before e except after c. Just deal with it.) It tasted good, but I sacrificed three feet of dental floss dislodging the chunks from amid my remaining teeth.

If Mom would've bought us braces, then I wouldn't get things stuck in between my teeth like ham bones, and you wouldn't whistle when you talk. But no, only our baby sister, Bun, got to have braces, and, and horseback riding lessons.

I digress. The next peice of candy that I ate was a turtle. When I was a kid, I'd catch turtles in Lake Charlotte and paint a number on their backs (no offense meant to Jerry). That way, I'd know if I caught the same one again. I always forgot what munber I used last. That's why there were so many 8s and 12s. So, when I see candy turtles, I go a little spastic. I put them aside, after I've numbered them.

Coran has decided to go to bed. She said that Aliens was giving her bad vibes. The-a-the-a-the-a-that's all, folks. Soon the sugar high will wear off and I want to be in bed before the downer hits. I'll identify myself before entering the bedroom.

I'm touring our grocery stores tomorrow with the corporate director. Maybe, I'll sleep under the bed tonight.

#####

Unsolicited, Brotherly Advice
(12-03-1998)

Hi Ricky,

I'm going to bed early. I'm not looking forward to going back to work at the middle school tomorrow. I definitely have a new-found appreciation for weekends.

Bun.

Good to hear from you, little Bun,

Mondays are a bummer. Especially the first one of the new school year. After a nice time with your family or just a day to yourself, it's hard to go back to a workplace full of people who are also trying to survive Monday. I hope you'll find your new job at the middle school to be bearable. It takes a break-in period, like shoes, blue jeans, a car or a husband. The middle school folks will need a break-in period too.

I'm confident that you'll learn from your past mistakes.

- Wear socks that match and have been laundered within the past month, and a blouse and slacks with the same qualifications. Remember to remove hair curlers and dental floss strands, and apply a double dose of deodorant before you leave home. Indulge in a breath mint or two.

- While entering the school building, use the doors on the right side, the ones that open inward.

- When you answer the office phone, don't put your finger down the front of your blouse while cracking your bubble gum and say, "Is this the person to whom I am speaking?" And don't follow up with a snort. Avoid storing that bubble gum behind your ear and retrieving it or cleaning out your ears with the business end of a No.2 pencil.

- Certainly the principal is a good person. Don't pass around notes with the office staff.

- While eating lunch in the cafeteria, use utensils and napkins even if the meal is chicken wings. Don't wipe off your fingers on your slacks. Resist the urge to start food fights when they serve peas and carrots as a side dish. Squelch your burps even though you enjoy the echoes and making the kids laugh.

- When leaving for the day, use the doors on the right side, the ones that open outward. Keep moving toward the parking area. Fight the impulse to turn around and flip off the school. Exit the parking lot before you rev the engine and pretend to squeal the tires on your Yugo.

Baby sister, these small steps should help to make your job bearable and keep you employed. I'm pleased to encourage you.

There are five Mondays next month.
Your big brother,
Rick

BEAUFURD
(12-04-1998)

Dear little sisters,

Do you remember our second cousin's brother-in-law's son, Beaufurd? He's the one who earned some prison time for trying to empty the 7-Eleven store's candy shelves into his trick-or-treat bag while dressed as the Lone Ranger and holding the clerk at bay with a realistic-looking cap gun loaded with fake silver bullets. He had a little too much to smoke at a Halloween party earlier that evening; the trigger for his crime.

Well, due to good behavior, he earned a night-shift job folding laundry for the prison's psychiatric wing. Maybe he was a prankster or perhaps just confused. Anyway, "The Boss" assigned him to fold a load of bedsheets into one-foot squares so that they'd fit through the slots in the metal doors. He spent the entire shift making the last fold to the left instead of to the right.

The next morning, the inmates couldn't open their sheets to remake their beds. To their credit, some of them got creative. They turned around and opened the bedsheets behind their backs where left becomes right and right becomes left. The incident nearly caused a riot. Unfortunately, Beaufurd was held to account, and now he's washing plastic utensils in the kitchen.

Little Ru, I'm sure you can understand the inference due to your recent wrist surgery. With your left hand unavailable for critical daily tasks such as shaving the left side of your body, perhaps you can use the imnates (got my m's and n's mixed up again) idea and accomplish some of your activities behind your back.

The warden and I were best friends as kids. He didn't appreciate being reminded of our boyhood pranks, which shaped his life and made him what he is today. You remember Phil Clink. He had a crush on you and still does. He reminisced about when you two danced along the shores of Lake Minnetonka. Too bad

122

you broke up that evening. He asked that I pass along greetings to his little "Mugwump."

Oh, I was talking about Beaufurd. I'll continue to do so if you promise not to interrupt me again. Sisters, I can never get a word in edgewise.

As his relative, Beaufurd believes that you owe him an apology. Due to Clink's memories of your breakup, you're partially responsible for the loss of his job. Sorry for waking you in the middle of the night with this email, but I thought you should know. I'll pass along your heartfelt sympathies.

I love sugar! This is without a doubt, probably the last time that I'll have a Rocky Road milkshake right before bed. Na Na, Na Na Na. I can't hear you. In answer to your thoughts, I don't care if you tell on me.

P.S. I didn't mention that Beaufurd is terribly allergic to lint. All of those early mornings trying to remove it from his hidden places so that he could sleep. His dad, Beaumount thought that the career potential was worth the price. He could've been a warden because that's where Clink started.

Phil gave Beaufurd two sets of bed sheets as severance pay. He's still laughing as the sheets were improperly folded.

Beaufurd got his revenge when he filled in one night at the main prison laundry. "The Boss" assigned him to do Phil's laundry. He hung the dress pants upside down in one of those clamp hangers. He laughed himself sick thinking that Clink would put his pants on upside down.

Life is sweet. I hope we can all rest peacefully now. Good night.

Rick

#####

POT-BELLIED PIGS
(1-16-1999)

Hi Ricky,

It's Saturday night, and I just spent another weird day with my friend Cathy. She would do anything for me. So, when she asked me to run errands, I gladly agreed. When she got to my house, she said that we had a 1:00 p.m. appointment in the toolies to visit pot-bellied pigs. (I'm not kidding.) She had decided her dog needed a playmate and she didn't want another dog.

So we found the dirtiest house I have ever seen. The lady not only has 40-some pot-bellied pigs, which go in and out of the house, but a cougar, a cougar-cat mix, and another exotic animal that's a combination of a racoon and something with a long, rat-like tail. She kept it caged because we were wearing perfume, which makes it aggressive. Phew!

Cathy wanted to hold all of the piglets and to know all of the facts. I passed because I was wearing a silk shirt and black jeans. I learned a lot, and I have to admit that some of them were cute. The big ones were small versions of the javelina we saw in Mom and Dad's backyard ... grotesque.

She kept saying, "Listen to the darling noises they make."

All the while I was thinking, "Look at all the hooey on my shoes."

When we got back in the car, her dog Vinnie had made a bed in my bucket seat. He sheds. Although I appreciated the warm seat, I then smelled like a blue heeler.

My bathwater is running. I just wanted to say, "Hi."

Was your day as fun?

###

Hi Ru,

How could my day be better than visiting a pot-bellied pig house? Reminds me of a frat-house dance that I attended in college, except that the women from S.O.W.S., the Sultry Obese Women's Sorority, not only had pot-bellies, but tube tops the size of tractor tires and L-cup, nickel-plated-underwire bras with a basement.

While the ladies hitchhiked to the party, truck drivers tried to pick them up, but there wasn't enough room in their cabs. Many arrived on flatbed trailers.

Every one of them wore a poodle skirt that was in reality a Rottweiler skirt with a doggy door. Underalls earned its name. Their legs hadn't been shaved since puberty, average age six. All had ankles that hung over their penny loafers, penny loafers that could hold a silver dollar and bobby socks named Ralph.

Several had palomino hair, ponytail weaves, and eyeglasses held in place by Superglue with lenses that made the limpid pools of their eyes look big enough to drown Godzilla.

They gnawed on Tic-Tacs the size of pecans, had braces on all five teeth, accompanied by lips that could stretch over a two-dozen-egg frying pan, and enough nose hair to braid a lariat.

The fraternity didn't offer a buffet because there wasn't a deli in the state that could supply that much tripe. Turns out that the ladies had been eating all day long. Eventually, the bevy of beauties released gas to such an extent that no one on campus dared light a match.

The twins Phil and I met had biblical names, Tirza and Hoglah. Tirzah wore a man's t-shirt that said, *Don't Make Me Kill You*, which only covered her neck. Hoglah had a pierced navel ring made from a chrome-plated hula hoop.

At night's end, the ladies offered goodnight kisses. Lenny Swartz lost a lung and part of his spleen because Eugeena liked to French.

The lion's share of the party goers visited the ER. The medical staff brought in plasma from all over the seven-county metro area. One of the girls, Bernice, had to be taken to the ER on a flight-for-life C-15 cargo plane. One of the pilots bailed out when Bernice let loose with the aftereffects of a seven-bean salad.

There were more incidents at that party that I won't share because the S.O.W.S. may find my comments to be insensitive. So, don't talk to me about how nasty it was visiting a pot-bellied pig house.

I don't know why I bother to reply to your emails. You always cause me to dredge up bizarre memories.

Your brother who will never pig out again,

Rick

#####

THE TWINS
(1-17-1999)

Dear sisters, Ru and Bun,

It's unkind of you to call me hugely weird because of my Pot-Bellied Pigs femail, which features S.O.W.S., the Sultry Obese Women's Sorority. Sisters who don't appreciate the subtleties of their brother's humor are rather boorish. Abnormally, the three of us are in perfect syzygy. I'm surprised to read that in this instance, our senses of humor differ. Well, I'm male and you two missed the boat.

That femail brought back the memory of my first double date. I invited Cathy and Sarah to a show at the 7-HI Drive-In Theater. I didn't get involved in the movie other than to learn the title, *The Green Berets*, and that it's a Vietnam war movie.

I hung the portable speaker onto my driver's-side window, went to the concession stand, and returned with a huge bag of popcorn.

Cathy, the blond, and Sarah, the red-head, had already climbed into the backseat of my 1967 Mustang where there was more room to mess around. I couldn't sit between them, but we made do because C&S had learned to cooperate with each other, being Siamese twins with one leg and a hip socket in common.

That was the first time I had been kissed by two girls at the same time. It was funny to pull off only three shoes and socks. What a spirited, memorable evening, accented by the sounds of mortars exploding, crunching popcorn, and playful screaming.

A drive-in employee knocked on my back window and yelled, "We're closed. Time to go home." I wiped the steam off of the side window and saw that we were the last car in the parking lot. The three of us got dressed, and I took the girls home.

Cathy still lives in Minnetonka. I haven't heard any news about Sarah's whereabouts. Since you didn't appreciate the nuances of my humor in the Pot-Bellied Pigs femail, you'll probably feel the same way about The Twins. I'm big-time bizarre because of my true-life, college-boy stories, and because you're girls.

I'm planning a date tonight with little wifey, the doubly gifted Cora Sue, C&S.

I wish I had a Mustang.

I hope all is well with you two.
Rick

#####

AHOE AND THE SKANK
(4-10-1999)

Dear little sisters Ru and Bun,

Ru, I'm pleased to hear of your successes at the new job. The boss already appreciates your expertise.

I'm sorry that you must meet with your ex, Ahoe, and his new wife, the Skank. During their visit, a grand piano will be dangling from a frayed rope outside of a 5th-floor office-building window, positioned above an old power pole with dangling, electrical wires, while the two of them are standing in a sidewalk puddle within the piano's shadow.

Just behind them lurks an open gutter grate. A gust of wind crosses it and flows up his loose-fitting, old-man shorts and her disgusting mini-skirt, spreading sewer gas that contains a virus known to cause untreatable, terminally itchy acne of the pelvic region.

Running their way is a big, honking, junkyard Pitbull named Zombie that hasn't tasted human flesh in two days.

Around the corner, a flatbed-trailer truck transporting a kiloton of ten-penny prickly-pear cactus needles, has veered off course heading towards their sidewalk puddle, the sewer grate, and piano shadow after avoiding the spent, jay-walking hooker whom Ahoe was checking out.

A 747 non-stop flight on its landing approach from Australia, during which every passenger had been served unfiltered, bottled Mexican swamp water, accidentally dumped its waste storage and a box of wooden matches above the piano.

Little sister, please avoid the immediate area, but remain within viewing distance. Greet them impolitely for me, verbally and with a time-honored hand gesture.

Your forgiving and forgetting big brother,

Rick

I nearly forgot, Hi Bun.

TUB TIME
(5-11-1999)

Dear lovely ladies,

After I took off my old black shoes, I complained, "Man, my feet are sore. No wonder those shoes were in the back of the closet covered in dust." My feet boasted more colors than a summer sunset. I thought, "It'd be sweet to do some tub time in a whirlpool bath and baby them." I tried strapping Cora's hand-held mixer onto the side of the bathtub in our master bathroom to churn the water, but I got my hair wound up in it. I didn't dare move it farther down the line. The best I could do was to dump hot water into the toilet tank, dunk one foot at a time into the potty, flush, and enjoy the swirl.

I'm six feet tall and I don't fit into that bathtub. It feels as if it's only two feet square. The tub doesn't hold enough water to cover all of my parts. No matter how I position myself, something gets neglected. In order to lay back with my head in the water, I have to bend my knees and park one foot on top of either side of the tub, but then my nose and ears fill up and the water level drops by two inches. No one wants to see me like that.

To soak my legs, I sit ramrod straight against the back wall of the tub, which boasts a temperature of 32 degrees Fahrenheit above the water level. I jump at the shock and strike my head on the towel rack.

Every frickin' time I step into the bathtub, I slip and nearly bust my ass on an oil slick of Cora's *Skin-So-Soft* bathwater treatment. I swear that it has a six-month, nuclear half-life. The last thing I need is another butt crack.

Cora often comforts, "Calm down. You haven't got enough butt to break, and there's certainly isn't room for another crack."

I've heard those insults more times than I can forget. I had to know. Tuesday evening before taking a bath, after I'd put on my bathtub spikes, I positioned her hand-held mirror and took a look at my backside. May I suggest to all beleaguered husbands, add that practice to your top ten Do Not Do List. From now on, Cora is not allowed in the bathroom when the moon is full.

Recently, while overnight in a hotel, I indulged in one of the advantages of hoteling: a half-an-hour shower.

I found a multi-faceted shower head mounted on the bathtub wall. I turned on the water, let it warm up, chose one of the eight shower-head settings at random, stepped in, and flipped the switch. Instantly, I found myself pummeled within an F-rated hurricane. The pulsating spray blew my hair back and decorated my chest and stomach with undulating divots. I won't attempt to describe the damage south of the beltline. You won't find water pressure of that magnitude at the bottom of the Mariana Trench. Real funny, Holiday Inn Express.

If I ever visit that hotel again, I'll flush the toilet as I climb into the shower. That lowers the water pressure without fail at home while I'm standing in our two-square-foot tub with my hair full of shampoo, and everyone in the family gets the trots. The shower reverts to a cold drizzle. I jump at the shock, smash into the shower accessories rack, and learn quickly if my shampoo has the no-tears formula.

Sisters, if your day has been stressful, relax, take off your shoes and enjoy some tub time.

Your big brother,
Rick

#####

OIL CHANGE
(8-30-1999)

Hi Bun and Ricky,

I just got home (7:15 p.m.). Had to go to the chiropractor and get an oil change, etc. My first day back to work was hugely busy, as I expected. My boss wants me to start training to do ads on the MAC and write copy. I have a two-day class the third week of September. She said it would be a good career move as they may need a third marketing officer if we merge or acquire more banks. I'd like that.

Dear Ru,

They'd be wise to take advantage of your proven writing skills, especially now that you've had your oil changed.

I didn't know that chiropractors do oil changes. Does he massage some of it onto your leather upholstery? Where do you keep your oil? Never mind, I don't want to know.

While he's at it, he could rejuvenate your spark plugs. It's for the best that he doesn't mess with your exhaust, but a new muffler is warranted.

Watch it! He may try to adjust your headlights or crack your trunk. Trunk, meh, all he'll find is a mini spare.

If you plan to get to know him better, ask about his manual transmission. Does he boast a four, six, eight, or is he one of those dangerous European models with a 12? Can he lay rubber in all gears or shift to 4-wheel-drive on the fly?

What about his cruise control? Does he know when to go slow?

Does he have a bench seat or a sporty bucket; a convertible top or his own hair?

Have a care if he asks to show off his moon roof.

As an adept writer, and a frequent patient, you could offer to create an oil-change advertisement for his chiropractic clinic.
Rick

LIQUOR
(9-08-1999)

Dear ladies,

Yes, we've decided to accept the transfer from Bristol, Wisconsin to Madison, Wisconsin, but we'll wait until spring.

You mentioned unusual names. I've got a few for your list, people named after liquor:

- Twin girls, Brandy and Gin.
- Twin boys, Seven and Seven.
- Hillbilly, Wild Turkey.
- Cowboy, Jack Daniels.
- Addicts, Rum and Coke.
- Hobo, Fuzzy Navel.
- Hispanic girl, Margarita.
- Gigolo, Screw Driver.
- Dean Martin's daughter, Martini.
- Viagra man, Pina Colada, straight up.
- Femme fatale, Daiquiri.
- Groin-damaged wrestler, Hi Ball.
- Woman with a little butt, Anisette.
- Grumpy old dude, Whiskey Sour.
- Psycho, Harvey Wallbanger.
- Northern enforcer, Canadian Club.
- Girl with a lisp, Wine Spritzer
- Same girl in prison, Wine Spritzer Cooler.
- Everyone's nanny, Liebfraumilch.

That's enough for now. I need a drink.

Your big brother,

Gin Rickey

AHOES
(11-05-1999)

Hi Ricky and Cora Sue,

I thought I'd better tell you about that last email from Bun. Her neighbors, Joy and Stan, showed up in Bun and Paul's new driveway saying the cops were going to be paying them a visit because their son egged Joy and Stan's house.

Bun and Paul told them that he was with them at the time their house was egged, and to go ahead and send the police. They'd rather talk to the police than them.

Then Bun said, "You want to be rid of us, and we want to be rid of you. So get out of our driveway and don't ever come back."

Way to sock it to 'em, Bun and Paul.

Ru

Dear Ru,

AMEN AND AMEN. Those folks are really a couple of AHOES. I'd love to punch Stan with an uppercut when I'm on my knees. That stick-chick Joy, stand her up in the county center and hang a flag on her face. I wouldn't egg their house but I'd whiz on it. Let 'em do a DNA test to see who did it.

Your POed brother,

Rick

#####

HAPPY BIRTHDAY
(11-12-1999)

Hi Ricky,
 I made you something for your birthday. I finished it today.
Fun!
Hope you're doing well.
 Ru

Dear little Ru,
 You're made me a birthday gift? I can hardly wait. The possibilities...don't tell me. Could it be a:
- Pair of skunk skin undies?

- Toy, Lone Ranger, six-shooter with real bullets?

- Pair of socks with cactus-pear thorns that show up after my shoestrings are knotted?

- Bottle of White Zinfandel that's actually hippo urine?

- Whoopee cushion with real gas?

- Toilet seat warmer coated with liniment?

- Giant-size can of Nestle's Quick laced with Ex-lax?

- Pair of eye patches backed with super glue?

- Faux-wool stocking cap made from nettles?

- Belt that's three inches short but marked at my waist size?

- Motion-activated Xena doll that sees me as the enemy?

- Pair of push-pin ear plugs?

- Narrow bike seat that rests on a pipe, which will pop through when I hit a pothole?

- Fragrant, after-shave cologne that attracts bats?

- Piano with 67 keys?

- Bathtub toy shark with hidden, wifely-programmable, six-inch teeth?

- Toothpaste laced with Prep H?

- Pair of tennis shoes that look right but are both left?

- Full-body mustard plaster?

- Year's supply of Lay's potato chips made with Olestra?

- Gallon jug of fresh-squeezed apple cider that's actually scented, cod liver oil?

- Visit from our old-neighborhood-bully Ricky Ahmet?

- Sneaked picture of Bun on a mountain-trail, nature call?

- Chance to go back in time and make the same mistakes again?

- Potted plant from the Addams family?

- Bag of bird seed made from uppers?

- Hyperactive sister with a black belt?

The possibilities are beyond my mere-mortal mind.

Your expectant, but not expecting, Big Brother,
    Rick

#####

RAJ
(12-10-1999)

Dear little sisters, RoboRu and Bun,

Fancy words intrigued me when I became an author. My writings appeared intellectual, and would've sounded so if Raj and I could've figured out how to pronounce those words. Later, when we reviewed the stories or I sent one of them to you, none of us knew what I was saying. I discontinued the practice and wrote with everyday words, such as "afraid" instead of "pusillanimous" when referring to discussions with Wifey.

I did come across a word that made sense to Raj and me: persiflage [n. PUR-suh-flazh]. If you're chatting idly with someone, passing the time with light conversation, you're engaging in persiflage. It's friendly, good-natured banter. Raj and I do this frequently. Even though I have two sisters and a wife, he's the only one who listens intently when I talk to myself.

We discuss a variety of subjects, and on occasion, we have different viewpoints, which can be healthy. I come away enriched and thankful for his understanding and patience; unlike my sisters, wife and psychoanalyst, Dr. Flemwadd, all of whom insist that I have multiple personalities, which are all weird.

Last weekend, during a heated discussion, Raj stomped out of the room unexpectedly. We haven't spoken since then.

Raj can get bent. There's plenty more personalities where he came from.

Your Big Brothers,

Rick

137

CORA HASN'T CHANGED
(2-12-1999)

Dear little sisters, Bun and RoboRu,

My three-day weekend is at an end. I'll be on the road for the next four days so thought I'd better send a note.

We received an invitation to the big boss's home in Vernon Hills, Illinois, for a party Friday evening. I bet he wants to meet Cora the Dish after hearing so many stories. He'd be better off playing rugby with a hornet's nest. I'm trying to decide if we should go.

Cora is a badass. She wears dresses on occasion, but always wears the pants. Her Harley doesn't register speeds below 70 m.p.h.

At dinner, she eats the skin off of the chicken. I've tried to convince her to pluck it first. She enjoys walking on my sore back Japanese-style, while wearing her golf shoes, the ones with composite spikes.

Cora plays tackle football. Her opponents have learned to forfeit rather than deal with sprains, strains, and broken bones— and Bret Farve is tired of getting goosed. She always loses. Twenty penalties for unsportsmanlike conduct doesn't win the game, especially in the first half.

I'm sick of eating oysters, rhino horn, spinach, swallowing blue pills, and getting bounced out of our waterbed five nights per week. What's wrong with just lying back and watching TV? Preferably *Xena the Warrior Princess*, not one of Cora's emergency-room-trauma shows. I'm already an experienced patient.

Cora's been sick this weekend, probably due to her penchant for wild-game sandwiches and chicken skin.

That's it! We're going to the boss's party. He deserves to meet Coran the Dishtroyer.

I hope all is well with my lovely femail relatives.

Your big brother, Rick

P.S. It's now 3-23-2020. Cora hasn't changed.

BO PEEP
(2-26-2000)

Hi little Ru,

It's your Bro. Where are you Ru?

I washed the garage floor today with Bo Peep Ammonia, lemon-scented. What a joke. Lemon-scented ammonia is like saying lilac-scented dead fish, or pine-scented litter box, or maple-scented compost heap, or rose-scented fart. It is what it is, and it stinks. At least I didn't have to wash my hands afterwards, because my skin was gone. As a result, I've been offered a job as a hands-stand-in for an upcoming horror movie.

I'd rather be an ass stand-in for Patrick Swayze, Jean Claude Van Dame or Crocodile Dundee. I'd have to shave it. No worries. I'll take a Bo Peep sitz bath.

Have you noticed that supermodels who throw their arms in the air have absolutely no armpit hair? They groom with Bo Peep.

I won't Bo Peep my feet because I'd lose my gig modeling for foot fungus ads, which only fit on wide-screen TVs.

Bo Peep is not for the squeamish, the Amish, or the Flemish. Those Flemish folks already have enough problems of their own. Who wants to be named after nasal discharge?

Ah, I digress, but from where; I'm not sure. Oh yes. Where are you, Ru? After such a lemon-scented femail, you shouldn't shun me, but instead reply, if you're able to Bo Peep the visuals.

Your Bro,

Keeping it clean.

I won't utter another peep.

#####

OUR NEW HOMETOWN
(4-01-2000)

Dear little sisters,

I'm excited about our new hometown and would like to share some of the highlights.

Last night, Cora and I met a few of the town officials, a diverse and mostly friendly group of people.

Town chairman Sod Omand Gomorrah shakes hands firmly, but stands too close while doing so.

Treasurer E. M. Besel is heavy set and has sticky fingers.

Secretary Jules Gayler is a congenial person with a limp handshake.

Chairperson of Cultural Diversity Frankie Vanderdyke has an iron grip.

Police Chief Buford Pusser carries a hickory stick, smiles and doesn't shake hands.

On another subject, the narrow, Little Litter River flows along the edge of town. Panfish daydream upon its surface. Even the youngest kids go swimming there because they float like corks. As an added feature, there are on-shore showers supplied by well water that's drawn from an aquifer nearly 80 feet below Joe Bob Styman's hog farm. We didn't shake hands with him.

The organic garbage-disposal plant is interesting. In addition to a landfill, it has several pools crammed with piranha. The director, Mr. Gimp Schmaldick, is also the principal alto soloist of the St. Peter's Church choir. He was busy wading into the ponds and scattering food waste. We didn't get to meet him.

The drug store, Snorts' Drugs, is a privately owned, 24-hour facility with a lunch counter. Inside the front door, there's a display of bottled bong water and a sign that reads, "A.D.D. children must be leashed." Regular customers believe them to be disruptive math students.

Drexel Spivey, the clerk, is lackadaisical. Customers who aren't standing in line sit at the lunch counter. Most are in a world of their own, chewing on complimentary mushrooms, and smoking.

The owner, L.S. Downs, spends a lot of time at the police station. We didn't get to meet him either.

I'll keep you updated once we become acclimated.

Your big brother,
Rick

#####

Mi Casa Su Casa
(7-16-2000)

Little sister Bun,

In answer to your inquiry, I've never watched nor have I been tempted to watch the TV show *Big Brother,* even though I cherish the title. As a contestant, I'd win the show because I'd get naked and would garner the entire female vote, except for my sisters and Wifey.

Will you be coming out here for Mother's birthday?

Your Big Brother,

Rick

Ricky,

Your sisters wouldn't watch the show under those circumstances. I will probably come to your place for Mother's birthday, Sunday-Tuesday. Are you and Cora going to be gone that whole time?

Bun

Dear Bun,

Unfortunately, we'll be gone. You're welcome to stay here. I'll set things up so you'll feel right at home. There'll be a pair of dirty, well-worn socks on the unmade bed with broken-in sheets, a partial can of Coke on the nightstand, and used toothpaste and a washcloth stuck to the sink in the master bathroom. The shower, tub and toilet will be in "as is" condition.

In addition:

- You'll find my ancient slippers next to the bed. Both of your feet should fit nicely inside one of them.

- I'll equip the bedroom with three-way light bulbs, and the TV with cable channels.
- The binoculars will be on the window sill. My neighbors may not be as entertaining as yours.
- Despite this hospitality, the fresh, homemade cookies are coming with me.

A word of warning: Beware of the bathroom mirror. It says mean things like:

- I don't want to see Big Brother. Keep the shower curtains closed!
- What's that in your teeth?
- Nice hair. Who do you think you're fooling?
- You'd better shave those ears or do a comb-over.
- You're blocking my view of the wall.
- Don't dare do that in here ever again.
- Go ahead and suck in your gut. It'll be back...momentarily.

Mi Casa Su Casa.
Your fully clothed Big Brother,
Rick

#####

RAMBLING
(5-06-2001)

Dear baby sisters, Ru and Bun,

I had a hankering for a meat dinner. The past few weeks, I've been dining on grapefruit, apple sauce, salads, ice cream, cookies, and well water. So last night, I fried a whopping burger and half a Vidalia onion, topped the burger with the onion, sweet pickles and cheese, and followed up with a fresh strawbaby sundae for dessert. And, I couldn't resist several fun-size candy bars. I started the meal with a beer, and as an after-dinner drink, another tall, frosty glass of A&W.

Son Jerry's new home has 1,800 sq. ft. I'm pleased that I have only two square feet. It's good that square feet are measured in two dimensions as my feet are too flat to be measured in three dimensions even though cubic feet sounds cool. My head has been observed in six dimensions, or maybe that's dementias.

I'm fortunate to have enough room between my flat-footed toes to house assorted structural deformities, garden dirt, and enough lint to knit a set of flannel jammies.

Earlier this week, I noticed that my socks were getting dirty, so I turned them inside out. That works with jockey shorts and undershirts too. When necessary, I put all of them into the wash hamper and go without.

I hang up my work shirt in the closet over the weekend. By Monday, it's ready to wear again.

Blue jeans are made not to wash.

Bath towels, once they're dry, there's no way to tell what I dried with them last week. And, I don't rinse the washcloth. That way I can lather up twice as fast next week when I shower again.

Q-Tips can do double-duty, if you use only one end per day. That allows time for the used end to dry for alternate days.

On occasion, I have to clean my electric razor. The other day, I had more whiskers after shaving than when I started. I emptied the contaminants into the bathroom sink, and followed up with a half-pint of Drain-O.

I'm glad that combs are cheap. I can throw away the ones I haven't lost after a few years. I took one of my childhood combs into the town barber. He stated that it contained hints Brylcreem and Butch Wax.

Last month, I discovered that we have transparent glass shower doors in our master bathroom. I could've been watching Wifey in the shower. I "cleaned" them, and when I'm home, she showers in the guest bathroom.

With the scraper and Mr. Clean still in hand, I washed the bathroom mirrors. I can see myself clearly. That's the last time I'll be "cleaning" them.

I moved on and scrubbed the sink faucets and handles, which revealed a label *Made in Germany of the finest lead.*

Our neighbor, Tom Peepin, informed, "The term 'miniblinds' doesn't imply that they shouldn't cover your entire master bathroom window. The view is interrupting my wife's evenings."

I replied, "Apparently, she doesn't need binoculars to take in my fine frame."

Perhaps in a former life, I was a Roman Centurion with two baby sisters. My name may have been Bodus O Sveltevus or Bestus Uv Siblingus or Smartus Uv Alluvus or Thirtysixius Flavious or Babeous Magneticus or Manicus Depressious.

That's enough rambling for now.

#####

RUSTIC
(6-04-2001)

Ricky,

It looks like we will be renting a two-room suite for Saturday night as the Torgesens don't want us to use their cabin.

Little Ru,

Relatives can be a pain in the bum. You're welcome to use my cabin, Shanty Shack, if you appreciate rustic. It doesn't have running water, but Quaking Aspen Creek is just on the other side of the railroad tracks.

The outhouse is original to Shanty Shack, 72½ years old, and still sitting (I left out the "h") on the same hole. Avoid whatever remains of the stack of Sears catalogs. Bring your own TP.

Inside the Shack, there should be a convenient Port-a-Potty, a 3-lb. Folgers coffee can. It was there last year.

The Shanty does not boast electricity. So what. The sunlight shines through the remaining pieces of glass in the window frames and dances off of the floating dust bunnies. The lack of window glass makes it easy to empty the coffee can with minimal splash back.

The romantic moonlight shines between the slats in the ceiling, enhanced as it passes through the clusters of spider webs.

Shanty Shack's spiders are night creatures. You won't notice them creeping about as you sleep soundly on the dirt floor. The earth is a constant 58 degrees, perfect for snuggling, although, I don't recommend getting naked. It's best not to entertain the hobos even though they gots no teeff.

Before retiring for the evening, consider sweeping the floors to rid them of any telltale Boone's Farm Strawberry Hill or Fuzzy Navel broken-bottle glass shards. The broom is in the outhouse.

#####

BOOK TITLES
(7-04-2001)

Dear little sisters,

You've suggested that I write a humor book about being me. I've been considering the idea and decided that I should first come up with a title for the book that I haven't written. Here are a few ideas:

- Sugar Buzz!
- What Women Want...Not
- Femails for the Fortunate
- Really?!
- Smell My Feet/Eat My Shorts
- That's Not Funny
- Cowbell is a Curse
- Close the Curtains
- I'm Telling: A Tell-All Book
- The ODDessy
- I Played Jarts
- My Parents' Only Biological Child
- How to Be Old and Not Know It
- The Inner Child on the Outside
- Booger Butter and Dingleberry Jelly
- Underpants, Who Kneads Them
- He is Not My Brother
- Hedgehogs Clog the Garbage Disposal
- The Oxford American Fictionary

- Wax Not, Want Not
- South of the Beltline
- Anything Two-ply is Reversible: A Guide to Financial Independence
- The How-to-Not-Write-Poetry Guide

Your Big Brother,
Rikki Tikki Tavi

#####

SCREAM
(9-07-2001)

Hi Ricky and Bun,

Mother left for home today. We had a lot of fun. She wanted to do everything, and we stayed up until midnight a couple nights watching videos.

I stalled going into work as long as possible after Mother got on the plane and even got my car oil changed first.

It'll be a full day tomorrow and then I'll have the weekend to recover from not much sleep as my neighbors were moving furniture again from 2-4:30 a.m. I wanted to pound on the wall and scream.

Hi Ru,

I'm pleased to hear that you and Mother had fun and made good memories for the both of you.

I'd like to meet your neighbors and get some advice on how to sustain 2½ hours of bed bouncing. I'd scream too. Although, I'd need a back brace, hormone shots, a kiloton of Viagra, a better mattress, and pre-planned funeral arrangements. Oh, and scatter my cremains back onto the bed so I can finish the last hour and a half.

Please check and see if your neighbors are seriously committed to their relationship. I'd be interested if all three of them are women.

Your big brother,
Rick

#####

149

IT'S ALL MY FAULT
(6-28-2002)

Dear little sisters,

I know, as a married man, no matter the occasion or the circumstance, that it's all my fault. For some reason, I felt compelled to compile a list of recent events that are all my fault. I'm sure that Wifey will not mind.

- The stock market fell because I invested my allowance last week.

- It's raining today because I didn't cut the grass yesterday.

- The Orkin man said, "You'd have fewer bugs if you'd weed the garden on occasion." Even that bugger is on my back.

- Our plumber stated, "I wouldn't see you as often if you'd eat more fiber." That guy is a real turd.

- Pastor Harms said, "Your confession isn't good for my soul."
  I thought, "To hell with you."

- Our son's bad knees are due to MY messed-up genes.

- The mechanic said, "Your alternator died."
  I replied, "So much for AC/DC."
  He added, "Your car needs a tune up. You drive too fast."
  I replied, "I can't drive 55. Forget it. You're too young to understand the references."

- Four of last night's six robo-callers who interrupted my supper said, "Unlisted numbers aren't much of a challenge."

- My urologist, Dr. Peebody, said, "That's a limp excuse. Prostate problems don't arise from eating irradiated fruits and vegetables."
  I thought, "Screw you."

- My proctologist, Dr. Gaez Pascer, said, "There's a planet named after you."
  I thought, "Up yours."

- After 31 years of happy marriage, Cora still holds me accountable for all of her pregnancies.

Little sisters, these listings made sense to me. If you don't understand them, I'm sure that it's all my fault.

#####

THIS AND THAT
(9-17-2002)

Dear little girls, Ru and Bun,

The circle of life continues at our home. I work to earn money to pay for my car repairs so I can drive to work. Hopefully, the aged Vegmobile won't require an additional arthritis injection during this fiscal year.

We refinanced our mortgage. Our first house payment isn't due until October 21st., which gives us time to recover from the Vegmobile's treatment. We negotiated an interest rate of 5.95%. It's not as good as your rate, Bun, but you smiled at the loan officer and he lowered yours to 5.65%. You should've flashed him and got your rate down to 4.65%. In this circumstance, I found both efforts ineffective.

Ru, I'm sure that you remember Salheptica and still take it along with Serutan. Serutan's ad soothed, "Gentle because it's Natures spelled backwards." Ru spelled backwards is Ur, a river in Russia.

I'd like to offer you ladies a word of warning about the hazards of grandkids messing around in your bathroom. When you arise in the middle of the night to brush your teeth and rid yourself of the remaining barbecue sauce from Tuesday's dinner, turn on the light. Otherwise, you may find that your botox lips have shrunk to less than their original size, resembling an old peach pit, thanks to the misplaced Preparation H. Not that this has ever happened to me.

Did you know that if you spread grapefruit juice on your face every morning for 21 days, you'll increase your chances by three-fold of earning early commitment papers? Not that this has ever happened to me.

Bun, I've learned from our mother that prior to your adoption, you were one of a set of triplets. The other two armadillos were

152

skilled at burrowing, eating ants, termites, and other vermin. Hopefully, you've overcome those temptations.

Cora sends her greetings and her apologies for this femail.

And that's the way it is.

I enjoy candy corn.

Your brother,

Rick

#####

ALL IS WELL WITH ME
(10-26-2002)

Ricky,

I just got home from the Women of Faith conference, which lasted late into the night and early this a.m. Nice, but way too long for me to sit in uncomfortable seats after sitting all day at work.

Time for a nap, but wanted to say Hi.

Little Ru,

Are they nuts staying up that late, or early? Are you sure they're the Women of Faith not the Women of the Evening? I don't want my baby sister's well-aged mind to be influenced by the wrong kind of people!

I, on the other hand, the left one, need not worry about such matters as my colorful memory engrams have faded into gray matter. My neural synapses are now wider than my nose. My mitochondria are hypochondria. And, doctors refer to my subatomic particles as quacks instead of quarks.

My fluid levels are mostly ice cream. My friendly intestinal bacteria have mutated into blue-green algae. And, I have esophageal reflux of the colon.

My nose hair grows up instead of down. My ear hair grows in instead of out. Therefore, and whatnot, my brain is being invaded by a forest of its own creation.

When I take a drug that has no side effects, my sides are the only body parts without side effects. Hormone therapy is of no value as it cannot find anything within me that hasn't already been screwed up.

So, as I lapse into Alzheimer's with shades of dementia, I need not fear having my well-aged mind influenced by the wrong kind of people.

###

A disquieting happenstance:

While searching for the correct turn-off road to a garage sale, I slowed down as I approached a steep hill with a hidden driveway. The motorist behind me was impatient, tailgating, and offering impolite hand gestures and vocalizations. I pulled over to allow Mr. Middal Fingas to pass by. As he did so, Sir Cussalot paused momentarily to offer his thanks in words not considered by Dr. Seuss.

While he was so engaged, a car came over the hill in no less of a hurry. The two spotted each other and waited until they came to rest in a local resident's front yard before exchanging pleasantries.

If I hadn't pulled over, I would be on a hospital bed exercising the remnants of my side-effected body parts through tubes and a mask, and communicating via Cora the Clairvoyant. She always knows what I'm thinking.

I hope you feel better knowing that all is well with me.

#####

In Vain
(11-06-2002)

Femail sisters, Ru and Bun,

Greetings from the most masculine of us all.

I understand that some folks make an effort to lower caloric intake, cholesterol count and the sludge in veins by ingesting EggBeaters instead of whole, wholesome eggs. As EggBeaters are egg whites, without egg yellows, I have a few questions on the value of eliminating yellow:

- Would calories, cholesterol, and sludge in veins be lowered by removing the yellow jimmie sprinkles on jelly donuts?

- Would bleaching yellow teeth enhance a multi-gapped-toothed smile?

- Would a coward be cowardly if he was considered "beige"?

- Would drivers actually yield if the yield signs were blood red?

- Would a double-purple line on the roadway prevent illegal passing?

- Would Dorothy travel to Oz without incident by following the puce-brick road?

Because the answer to all of these questions is a resounding perhaps, and the efforts, likely in vain, I'll continue to add one whole, wholesome, non-organic, grocery-store-fresh, raw egg to each of my homemade, chocolate, banana, root beer milkshakes.

P.S. Tuesday, I dined on turkey instead of beef, keeping my cholesterol count low.

My dear feminine omnivores, on another sisterly subject: Ru, is your chosen nickname for Rhonda. If your name was Beulah, would you choose Bu as your nickname, Fluenza, Flu, Neutera, Neu, Tululah, Tu Lu, Duelene Duvou, Du Du or Caty Caren, Ca Ca? You're a Wehler by birth, so Fatima Assandra wouldn't be appropriate.

Bun, is your chosen nickname for Sandi. It's best not to go there. The same is true for Rick, my chosen nickname for Richard. As with Ru, our nicknames could easily be taken in vain.

#####

SALTY
(11-25-2002)

Dear little Ru,

In the past, I dusted our living room end tables Saturday morning, and by Monday evening, I could autograph them as if they were Picasso artworks.

It seems that our new air filter is working. I gave the end tables a dusting on Tuesday, and the only thing I signed on Thursday was a contract for the room that Cora reserved for me at the retirement home.

It's dry in the house, so I activated the humidifier, but haven't as yet reset the water softener since Andy and family moved out. The softener recycles more often than needed for two people (soon to be one people?) making the water salty. The humidifier vaporizes so much salt with the water that when the sun shines through the windows, it hits the salt crystals in the air, and the rooms look as if disco balls are hanging from the ceilings. It's pretty but now I'm always thirsty, and haven't had to season my French fries.

Your Big Brother,
Rick

Dear Big Brother,
Only you, Ricky. Only you.

#####

158

DEFORMITIES
(11-28-2002)

Lovely Sisters,

Recently, when I had a physical, the doc asked how I got the scars on my arm. I've not heard a believable account of that childhood event. She also questioned my wandering left eye, unmanageable emotions, oversized flat feet, gray hair on the back of my head that resembles a paint stripe, and my addiction to sugar and women. Perhaps you have some explanations. I'm waiting. No hurry. I'm waiting.

I told Ms. Doc that I earned the scars during the filming of *Dina Phobia*, an adult-rated version of the dinosaur classic, *Dinatopia*. A pterodactyl swooped down to grab the heroine, the innocent Dina Dosit, who wore only a lei and a seductive smile.

I intervened and Ptery slammed into my character, Matta Hairy, a South Seas Islander, sporting long, braided, black hair; bare chest, legs and feet, and a huge loin cloth.

I blasted the mechanical flying dinosaur with a flamethrower, which Matta Hairy kept on hand for just such occurrences. Some of the propellant stained my loincloth.

While wiping up the overflow, the makeup artist, Miss Lelu, tipped over the bottle of Jack Daniels our director had set aside as he lit a joint. His booze caught fire, as did his chair and surroundings, and my flamethrower arm and loincloth, the sight of which caused my left eye and my emotions to go screwy, permanently.

Dancing about and stomping the blaze blessed me with oversized, flat feet. The gray stripe on the back of my head arose from ash stains.

All seemed worthwhile because Dina Dosit visited me often in my lanai, adorned in her lei and seductive smile. She spoon-fed me ice cream, pastries, candy, and other sweets. She smiled seductively and I got lei-ed. Thus, my addiction to sugar and women.

This account is rooted in fact, just like the tales I spin about you two, my spinster sisters.

I hope that you have a Happy Thanksgiving.

#####

WE BOTH WEAR THE PANTS
(12-12-2002)

Little sisters,

Why is it that people in our family, over the generations, routinely marry controlling mates? Perhaps because we were all raised in such an environment? As a teenager, I promised myself that I would not become a controlling personality or succumb to a woman of that sort. I'm pleased that Cora and I both wear the pants in our family and share the responsibilities.

Currently, I'm in charge of the house-cleaning, laundry, pet grooming, and political activism. As it's October in Wisconsin, soon I'll add snow removal to my domain.

Cora says that my mind is one of a kind. Therefore, I command our intellectual properties: the stories that I continue to write, femails, and my garage-sale clothing. Tomorrow, I'm going to wear a recent purchase, boxers instead of briefs.

I have to sign off now as reruns of *Friends* are soon to begin. Cora feels there is much I can learn from Joey.

We both wear the pants!

#####

MINT DESSERT
(12-22-2002)

My dear little sisters Ru and Bun,

I'm emailing in earnest, hoping that this communication finds you at home and in good physical, emotional, and mental health after your travels ... however unlikely.

The visit of such a pair of female relatives and your progeny during these past few days has made me proud to proclaim that I've never considered polygamy. Due to your plotting and planning, I've regained three pounds of my hard-fought weight loss. You two are well aware that mint dessert does not readily pass through my digestive tract, but instead, adheres, for a time, to the most unflattering parts of my body, like rust on a chrome bumper. I will assuredly remember and appreciate your loving gift in the near future as I enter the bathroom and try to decide whether it's better to stand, sit, or kneel.

Bun, at the end of the month, I'll enjoy our enhanced cable bill. Our nephews, your sons, must not have realized that the 800-numbered cable channels on our TV service are pay-per-view, and documented. I'm sure the cable company welcomes viewers willing to pay for such delights as *8-Legged Freaks* and *Virtual Virgins*.

Ru, your grandbabies are so cute. I loved speaking to them softly while I carried them about the house, taking in the sights. I'll be reminded of our time together until the next laundry day.

Your daughter was so kind the first evening of your visit. She smiled unconsciously at my every humorous anecdote.

Your long summer's walk with Cora, while your daughter rested, will strengthen Cora's body after she recovers from dehydration.

Ru and Bun, your unsolicited praises of my garage-sale story, and your assurances of its publication, have inspired me to rewrite it.

I must sign off quickly, thanks to the mint dessert.

Your always loving brother, be sure and come back soon,

Rick

#####

Oogmat of Lake Charlotte
(2-09-2003)

Dear Bun,

I came across this email recently, your origin story, on which the poem, "With Love for Bun," is based.

###

Little Bun,

I'm sure that if you'd spoken in full confidentiality with Mother, she would've told you candidly about your first adoptive parents, a pair of armadillos, and their untimely demise.

They passed on together, quickly, as the septic service truck that flattened them had tandem wheels. Your parents were roto-tilling the beaches in the heavens by the time the second set of tires rolled over them. Mother gathered their remains and sprinkled them between the rows of her petunia garden.

I don't believe Mother knew much about your life before she found you sniffing around in her petunias even though sightings of a small, blonde creature hunting in the weeds and dining on frogs and salamanders were common in the Lake Charlotte neighbor-hood.

The Marks family, who lived kitty-corner from our place, on the shores of Lake Charlotte, called animal control whenever they spotted you foraging along the water's edge. After Mother brought you home, (Dad had little say in the matter) you exacted revenge on the Marks by emptying the contents of their garage into the lake.

Without your competition for food, the muskrat population increased many fold. They took over your burrows and dug many of their own into Mr. Fensted's shoreline, another unhappy neighbor.

While fishing at Lake Charlotte, you were the only local who could unhook a bullhead without harming it or getting impaled by its sharp fins.

You taught the ducklings how to swim. Only the strongest were able to keep up due to your large, webbed feet.

Mother said that the bald spot on the back of your head came from your powerful legs as you pushed yourself across the carpet while lying on your back. Actually, that was the last hair to grow back in after the physicians removed your armadillo plating.

I'd wished that your bedroom was in our unfinished basement as was mine. On the few occasions that you camped down below, the crickets' songs were little more than dinner bells. While you pigged out, I slept soundly.

It's still said, nearly 35 years after your departure, that Lake Charlotte's amphibian population has yet to recover.

There are other tales about Oogmat of Lake Charlotte that Mother wouldn't have shared with you. Those will have to wait for another time when you've matured.

May you continue to thrive, little Oogy.

Your only brother,
Rick

#####

HAPPY BIRTHDAY TO BUN/OOGY
(6-24-2003)

Dear little Bun/Oogy,

I'm emailing you this birthday greeting from our community's psychoschizoidotic repository. I'm doing so now as there are times when milliseconds, days, and weeknights disappear without asking my permission. In case that happens on your actual birthday, please accept this singing femail today.

Happy Birthday to Bun.
Happy Birthday to Oogy.
Happy Birthday to you two.
Happy birthday to U.

This card may be less enjoyable if you knew where I'm sitting within the psych cell and what I'm wearing.

I remember when you two were little; we'd go trick-or treating. You'd wear princess masks, which prepared me for dating two of the Finley quints, the conjoined ones, Cathy&Sarah a.k.a. C&S.

As a toddler, you caught and dined on toads, salamanders, and bullheads, which also prepared me for dating the Finley quints, the unconjoined ones.

I remember the bald spot on the back of your head from carpet burns just like, well you know.

Actually, some of the identical Finley quints were quite pretty, if you looked at their reflection in a mirror so all that the parts lined up properly.

I hope that you appreciate how you've enriched my life and damaged C&S. They were ultimately spoiled for all other men who couldn't measure up to my standards.

Cora stated, "From now on, me, myself and I, will be the only threesome you'll experience."

Sorry, I got deviated from my original purpose of wishing you a happy birthday. I'll sing you a song before the repository's suppository specialist inflicts my medication.

In agadda Davida, baby.

No that's not it.

Jeremiah was a bullfrog, he was a good...

Nope.

Oh, happy day! Oh, happy day!

That's closer.

Happy Birthday to Bun.
Happy Birthday to Oogy.
Happy Birthday to you two.
Happy birthday to U.

Sincerely,
Richard Alan Wehler, son of Gerald, son of Erv,
son of Gustav, son of Gustav.

#####

USHER
(7-28-2003)

Dear Ru,

You've got talent. I'm pleased that others besides your brother and lust-struck teenage boys recognize it.

I'm asked to participate in the theater on occasion, but unlike you, not as Donna. Instead, an Alzheimer's victim, a troubled child transplanted into an old man's body, a stand-in for Lennie Small in *Of Mice and Men* when he gets shot, and a crime victim covered in facial bandages, tubes, electrodes, and catheters.

Once, in my early thirties, when I was a body-builder, weighing 205 pounds, stacked six feet, one and a half inches tall, I was offered a role as the stud in a porno foursome. Cora decided against it. I dreamt a totally unforgettable performance.

In the meantime, I'll continue my current theatrical gig, an usher (not the R&B Usher), at Dudley Riggs' Brave New Workshop.

Your brother, who can put on an act,
Rick

#####

ALL FOR THE PRICE OF A T-SHIRT
(9-13-2003)

Dear Ru and Bun,

Cora and I are leaving this morning for her Ma's place in northern Minnesota. We didn't feel like getting up early, so we're taking our time and we'll get there later today.

It rained hard last night, and now just enough to keep the ground wet. The grass will grow in time for it to freeze to death.

I've had a t-shirt made with Cora's picture on the frontside. I wear it as a night shirt. That way, popular or not, no matter where I sleep, Cora will be there with me. Fortunately for her, I sleep on my back.

Recently, based on my success, I've had several other t-shirts made, each featuring one of this bevvy of beauties: Xena the Warrior Princess, Jennifer Lopez, Charlize Theron, Liv Ullmann, Bella Abzug, and the former US attorney general, whose name escapes me, as with so many others.

The t-shirt jammies work well. The ladies have always enjoyed our bedtime activities; and there's no grousing about cold feet, toenail length, snoring, and bed-cover theft. They're eager for my company. Complaints about headaches or PMS are nonexistent. They don't spoil the moment by uttering such inappropriate comments as:

- What did you eat for dinner at that business meeting, bean burritos?

- Call the neighbors and tell them to shut up that dog.

- Shower and shave first.

- The headboard is rattling.

- Time out. Hand me the remote. I hate *Star Trek*.

At their insistence, my t-shirts are stenciled in the comment balloon above the ladies' pictures with, "Oh Baby, You're the Best."

All for the price of a t-shirt. (I have a CD player that provides surround-sound cooing.)

The t-shirts have other applications. On occasion, I'll wear one of my femme-fatale jammie-shirts while on a long drive. That way, I have company in the front seat. Jennifer compliments my driving ability and sense of direction. If I hit the brakes, Charlize is there to cushion me. Liv never changes the radio station during a Led Zeppelin toon. Bella laughs at my witticisms. The former Attorney General doesn't mention politics. And, bathroom stops have decreased to single digits.

At times, I'll wear one of the t-shirts while dining. The lucky lady on hand acts as a napkin; and her smile is ever present. There's no comments about speaking with my mouth full, or complaints when I fill my face with whipped cream right from the can instead of baptizing the chocolate pudding. She listens intently to my garbled, dinnertime gab.

I could continue ad infinitum, but two more examples will suffice:

- They girls fight to accompany me to the gym, and the winner is pleased to pat dry my forehead.

- They keep me company while I'm at the computer without offering corrections to my diction.

All for the price of a t-shirt.

Your traveling brother, I brought my jammies,
Rick

#####

ME AND KIDS
(9-21-2003)

Ricky,

Sounds like you had a good time with the kids. It's no surprise to me that they relate to you. They always have. Another gift of yours.

Ru,

Thanks. On second thought, are you just picking on me like when we were kids because I was a boy and you weren't ... mostly? You could punch like Ali, and you'd tell Mom on me if I punched you back because she said I wasn't allowed to punch girls. Since I've been married to Cora, I've often wondered if you two knew each other when you were children.

You're right, though. I do get along with kids, until they're old enough to know better. Here are some reasons why.

We:

- Are of similar emotional age.

- Like to play the same games: *Chutes and Ladders, Hide and Seek, Peek-a-Boo, Steal Your Nose*, and *Fart Noises.*

- Like to mess around with bugs and frogs.

- Have the same tastes for food. It must be easy to chew, spoonable, and saturated in sugar. We hate veggies, especially broccoli, peas, and lima beans. Plus, it's best to cut our grapes in half.

- Have the same overnight habits: bathroom trips, hungry at midnight, thirsty at 2 a.m., and we need someone to snuggle.

- Ask similar questions concerning the opposite sex: Does she have girl germs? Does he have cooties?

- Are afraid of the dark and the monsters under our bed or in the closet.

- Sneeze at the wrong moment: with a mouth full of anything, while going potty, when getting a smooch, or a flu shot.

We:

- Ask Mom to explain weird words that we hear in movies or from friends.

- Don't like punishments: no TV or toys, time-outs, and sitting on the chair.

- Think that changing out of dirty clothes, tying shoestrings, and jammies with feet are all stupid.

- Dislike chores.

- Should be allowed to stay up and watch late-night TV shows.

- Think that it's more fun to take a bath with company.

- Are still perfecting potty skills.

- Are strong like the Incredible Hulk or Superman so don't mess with us. Look at our muscles.

These are just a few of the reasons why I get along with kids. I'll send more later. Right now, I've gotta go potty before Cora sees me holding myself shut.

#####

RYAN, WOMEN AND ME
(3-28-2004)

Dear little sister, Bun,

Bun, it's your fault for birthing Ryan, a babe magnet. Mother and I were talking about him last night. You're going to have your hands full. The girls have liked him forever because he's not afraid of them, unlike me. But, at age 15, maybe he's not interested yet.

Females are primitive creatures, able to sense fear. They smell it, feel it in the air, relish it like a Black Mamba, and strike without mercy. But, maybe Ryan won't date.

He's friendly and communicative, which is difficult for me when my mind is in a blur. But, maybe Ryan won't go steady.

He has an innocent look, wide eyes, and a kind smile, which I'm unable to master while sweating profusely, shaking, and searching for the door. But, maybe Ryan won't get engaged.

He's open and shows his feelings. I do that too, but primal fear is not a sought-after quality. But, maybe Ryan won't get married.

My best wishes go out to him. I hope that one day Ryan may be willing to instruct me in the ways of womankind, so that I may die in peace, not fearing that God may be female.

Your brother, who's nearly not afraid of his wife and sisters,
Rick

#####

DRIVE-TIME RADIO
(4-19-2004)

Dear little sisters, Ru and Bun,

I listen to a radio station on the drive to work that's based in the small town of Deforest, Wisconsin, no doubt named by an 1800s Norwegian lumberjack.

The station specifies its location, "93.1 on your dial," followed by the sounds of waves lapping a shoreline, and the slogan, "The Lake." The waves must be in their toilet tank because the only reasonable-sized body of water within miles of Deforest is the manure pond situated on a local dairy farm.

Their intro should be: "93.1 on your dial," followed by cattle mooing and the slogan, "Come on down to defarm." Instead of classic rock, they should float polkas on the airwaves.

I've come across their incestuous sister station while driving in Chicago, "96.9 The Ride." When the DJ shuts the hell up, the station plays 1960s classics.

There's no way to have "The Ride" in Chicago traffic. It's a flipping, mind-altering, migraine-producing, prostate-swelling, death-defying practice in self-defense and anger management.

They should rename their station, "96.9 The Bird." Imagine the free advertising on the tollways. Plus, the DJs could shout, "The Bird is the Word" or "Flip 'em the Bird."

For certain, this femail will earn a spot on your top ten list.

Your big brother,

Rick

174

PARADE OF HOMES
(6-12-2004)

Little ladies of the feminine persuasion,
  I send you greetings from the realm of hunkdom.
  Cora had freebie tickets to the Parade of Homes pre-opening gala, due to her prestigious position as a loan officer. So, much to my disappointment, we attended the event.

There was lots of food, mostly inedible, gourmet, finger sandwiches, and fancy little desserts, served under a big tent sheltering 400 guests and a sign stating, Capacity 150. Cora and I had a beer.

We toured several crazy-expensive houses featuring 6,000 sq. ft. and more of living space, a myriad of windows, bathrooms, stone countertops and fireplaces, hardwood floors, and stainless steel appliances.

The first house we visited covered an entire lot with a tad of green grass in the "courtyard." Even if we could afford such a mansion, we wouldn't.

We don't need a 400 sq. ft. bathroom with half a dozen windows. Although I'd take on the challenge, I probably couldn't stink up that much space. How many mirrors does one person need while seated? Wave at the neighbors while taking advantage of the walk-in shower that brags enough nozzles to clean a 4-wheel-drive pickup truck, complete with an under-chassis flush. The bathtubs are big enough for a congregational baptism. I prefer the more intimate one-person tub shared with Cora.

I bet they had to slaughter three giant redwood trees and a herd of cattle to create the staged furniture on display throughout the homes, including the bathrooms.

If I had emptied every shoe I've worn during my childhood, 54 years thus far, and saved all of the pebbles and sand, I couldn't construct a square foot of one of the thick granite countertops. If we were to pay beaucoup bucks for such a weighty extravagance, it'd move with us to our next home. Cora would have to lift it.

There are fireplaces everywhere, except the closets.

Perhaps the three-story great room is necessary for the kids' fenced-in trampoline.

One of the children's rooms has a ladder and a swing mounted into the ceiling. A two-year-old would climb to the top of the ladder and then call 911 from his personal cell phone. I've heard of basket swings suspended in adult bedrooms, (I wouldn't mind owning one) but not in a child's room. The little one will launch himself out of the swing, through the bedroom door, into his well-windowed bathroom, avoiding the fireplace, all the while waving to the neighbors.

The houses contain enough plasma TVs to deplete the entire Madison Red Cross emergency system. The TVs were playing videos of glaciers calving with voluminous stereo impact. Not a good thought for Wisconsin residents.

There were instructional signs in front of every house that read, "No High-Heel Shoes Please." Interesting in that the invitations informed the fortunate attendees that said event is semi-formal. Perhaps the president of the construction company has a thing for feet.

Those who gave a rip, such as me, left their heels at the entrance and chose a better pair on the way out. I had cut the grass barefoot before heading for the gala. They gained little by my courtesy except for the green footprints on the trampoline.

There's not a climbing tree, a yard for playing catch, or a sidewalk for hopscotch within the neighborhood—only streets and alleyways for car accidents and decorative ponds in which to farm carp.

Cora will not be recommending a new home in this market-place to her clients.

We stopped in at a few garage sales after the gala with no success, and then visited the annual Sun Prairie Art Fair in the Park. There was more room in the park than in the homes we visited, but way fewer bathrooms. The fair was packed with vendors. Half of them were selling food. The rest were offering artful wall plaques with sayings like: "I'm your brother and there's nothing you can do about it." I bought two.

All of them offered directions to the bathrooms.

When Cora and I returned to our modest home, I reached up and touched the hallway ceiling, set my two plaques onto the laminate kitchen countertop, and opened the living room window. I turned on our box-style TV, and we leaned back in our garage-sale recliners to watch Vanna.

The next morning, Cora went shopping for a bedroom swing, and I took the opportunity between rainstorms and mosquito swarms to cut the grass for the third time this week.

Two houses sold on our street recently and the new families are moving in today. We haven't met them yet even though they're out in their front yards. I hope they'll stay put.

Thanks, Ru, for the Red Lobster gift card for Cora's birthday. We went there for dinner two nights ago. The card paid for Cora's dinner and she paid for mine.

Your big brother,
Rick

#####

THE TASTE OF MADISON
(9-04-2004)

My dear little ladies,

There's a big festival going on locally called "The Taste of Madison." (I wonder if Madison tastes like pistachio.) I'll ask Cora to take me along. Usually, she doesn't appreciate my company because an all-day event on my timetable is an hour and fifteen minutes.

Cora is content to walk around, enjoy the sites, the vendor booths, and the people, while I'm impatient and thrifty. I won't stand in line to buy beer in a plastic cup for $12.50. It's most likely Bud's third label and half of it is foam. Or pay $6.50 for a brat, a hunk of ground-up pig lips and cheap spices packed in a gut casing.

I'm not walking up to that ice cream booth. By the time I make my way through the crowd, I'll have been pushed, shoved, sneezed on, and felt up by three dozen people, all of whom were extras in the Freddy Krueger movies. Besides, that's not ice cream. It's "kwikcrete." It's pliable at first, but tomorrow. I'll need a crowbar.

There's plenty of jewelry for sale. It's amazing what the vendors create out of glass, aluminum pull-tabs, and painted fingernail clippings. Each selection is priced well beyond the reach of my monthly allowance.

Then there's the short, overweight, newlywed couple. The bride shouldn't wear low-rider, hip-hugging yoga pants. The groom should bury that orange wife-beater, no-armpit t-shirt. I've seen less body hair at a Clydesdale exhibit. I'm thankful that I didn't eat a brat.

The air reeks. Many members of the crowd are smoking cigarettes, cigar turds the size of cruise missiles, and ganja. There's enough smog to set off any self-respecting fire alarm; and the breeze blows in my face no matter which direction I walk. I'd rather attend a dairy expo. Distant music continually invades my skull. My tastes don't include Hip Hop, Rap, or Oldies played by oldies trying to be youngies.

After we arrived home that evening, I had a milkshake, and slept in the closet beneath my Davy Crockett blankie.

Your big brother,
Rick

#####

NEW YEAR'S EVE
(12-30-2005)

My dear, sweet little Ru,
    I am working a lot, just like you.

    Cora and I are going to dinner on New Year's Eve.
    With no liquor, my parts, I won't need to relieve.
    No one had better make a sound or a peep,
    'cause I'm going to bed early for a full night's sleep.
    As one day off from work is not nearly enough,
    Hey, I think for a change, I will sleep in the buff.
    Yes, for a sister that's too much information,
    But for one I hope, it will be an inspiration.
    So the night could be a year-ending dream.
    No, if I bother Cora, she'll rupture my spleen.

    Happy New Year from your big brother Rick

#####

BIKE SEAT
(3-06-2005)

Dear Little Sisters: Ru and Bun,

I'm excited to try out my new, equipment-friendly, bivalve bike seat. It resembles two Little League catcher's mitts separated by a spread-eagle pipe.

Setting my butt cheeks on those little mitts would be like outfitting Dolly Parton with a training bra, or Chuck Norris and Sylvester Stallone with BB gun pistols.

I'm sure you're interested in further analogies:

- Fitting my feet into a pair of Wifey's shoes. (I'm sure she has a matching purse.)
- Pouring a pot of tea into two demi-tasse cups.
- Hulk Hogan and Arnold Schwartzenegger bunking on futons.
- Quelling a migraine headache with a baby aspirin and a kiss from Mommy.
- Peeing into a 2oz. cup at the doctor's office.
- Plugging silver dollars into the Tony the Tiger bank that I found in a 12oz. box of Frosted Flakes, the one with the Find Tony the Tiger maze on the back panel. (I never could get to that toothless bugger.)

I'm suited up and I'm going to give it a go. Upon my return, I trust that our emergency-care health insurance will pay to repair my friendly equipment.

#####

BUTT OF THE JOKE
(1-01-2006)

Dear little sisters, Ru and Bun,

Bun, our parents conspired and unfairly made you years younger than Ru. To add insult to injury, they endowed you with a butt. That was flat-out unkind.

Cora said, "Hubber, girls like guys with a nice butt. Looks like I'm out of luck."

While I'm sporting jeans, the only ways to tell the front from the back are the zipper and belt buckle.

I can avoid unkind comments by wearing a large-tall shirt with its tail hanging out or by remaining seated. Although, without a derriere, chairs are uncomfortable.

When I lose my balance and fall down, which, due to my inherited lack of coordination is a common occurrence, I make an effort to face-plant.

It's common in today's styles to have a "catch phrase" displayed on the backside of jeans. I'm developing "butt-of-the-joke" stencils for the less fortunate.

- It Is In Here
- Butts Aren't All They're Cracked Up to Be
- The Tragedy of Liposuction
- I Can't Make an Ass of This
- Yes, I Can Sit Down
- Proctological Nightmare
- Sport Saddle

- UNIBUTT
- Coming or Going?
- Flat Yuleance I'll use this one during the Christmas season.
- Cop a Feel? Don't Give Up.

Little Ru, feel free to take advantage of my "butt-of-the-joke" ideas.

Your underprivileged brother,
Rick

#####

THE GOURMAND
(12-17-2006)

Dear lovely ladies,

Cora the Dish and I enjoyed ourselves at the corporate dinner in Minneapolis last Friday evening. We dressed in semi-formal attire for the function. Cora looked delicious in her little black dress with a V-neckline, revealing just enough cleavage to keep me gawking. Most of the other attendees were in casual apparel, which earned the Dish a fair amount of surreptitious glances.

Afterlife's, a gourmet restaurant, served us a five-course meal. Their maître d' introduced each course with a speech in his contrived French accent. It may seem like a lot of food, but not so much.

The first dish was an oyster mushroom bisque, a thick, dark soup served in a large flat-bottomed bowl. There was barely enough barf to cover the bowl's base and coat my throat in gawd-awful, luke-warm, dead fungus.

The next course was swordfish, pronounced with the w. The plate, as big as a pickup-truck hubcap, mourned a dollop of fish, a round, ¼-inch-thik slice the diameter of a silver dollar, lying in state on a bed of greenish bile.

The following decedent was a puny piece of pink pork served on the same mortuary platter as the swordfish. It rested peacefully on a bed of rice and pasta mixed with an unpronounceable liquid cheese, which must have been created by chef Vlad from Transylvania.

The main course was a nearly departed New York strip steak. If we were to dine at a New York strip club, and the waitress wore only something of a similar size, I wouldn't tip her an extra nickel to remove the crepe nose cozy. Our dessert was a fancy pudding, christened with caramelized sugar, deemed creme brulee ä la mort.

The waiters served each course with a different vintage of wine, which to be polite, I drank. I didn't notice that the meal took three and a half hours to complete, or that I had consumed fewer calories in food than in wine.

We had taken our leave before a sloshed lady shed her casualwear, danced to non-existent music, heaved up her swordfish, accompanied by the greenish bile and several vintages of wine, and baptized a few admirers.

We pulled into a parking lot along the way to the hotel. I took off my sport coat and tie; Cora kicked off her heels; and we ran into a Dairy Queen, and pigged out.

Your Brother Rick,
The Gourmand

#####

ENGAGED
(11-30-2007)

Dear little sister Ru and her lucky-dog fiancé Terry,

Little Ru, you have hair the color of a lion's mane, the eyes of a lemur, the smile of the Cheshire cat, powerful arms likened to a three-toed sloth, legs with the agility of a cheetah, and the feet of a mountain gorilla.

A sheik would offer me his entire harem in trade for such a treasure. You engaged yourself to Terry and I got nothing in return. You're such an animal.

Those privy to the private communications between brother and sister will know that Ru understands her brother. She's skilled at separating his awkward reality from his flights of fancy, like a colander that retains the counter-clockwise rotini while allowing the mishmash to pass through.

Terry, any twisted comments spoken by Ru's brother due to the influence of complex sugars and the lingering effects of congenital oxygen deprivation, should be taken seriously, along with the attributes previously listed. Best of luck to you.

Rick

#####

A DRESS
(12-02-2007)

Ricky,

I need a dress to get married in. Do you have some I can choose from? Online shopping is like having the store be your personal shopper. You try on the dresses and then bring them back to the store. You never know what will fit or look good on you.

Little Ru,

I understand completely. Although I haven't gotten married recently, I have participated in a few ceremonies. At times, I'm not sure how much leg to show. Styles change more quickly than my taste.

I do have an ensemble in mind. The dress is an elegant, yet subtle, deep blue with a low back, just a bit risqué. It's V-neck plunge requires some waxing. The length falls a pleasant halfway between knee and ankle with a right-side slit that ascends midway between knee and hip. Considering our height difference, the dress will need some alterations.

I've had a difficult time finding size thirteen heels of a modest height with serpentine straps in a complementary color, but you're three sizes smaller than I so hopefully there's more availability.

The clutch's color matches the dress. It has enough embedded jewelry to be noticed as a classy accessory.

If you'd like, I'll address your concern with Se'arg and ask for a consultation.

Baby Sister Ru,

Your plan to recover from arthritic surgery by next summer is a great encouragement for any hurting person to follow in your footsteps. You've staved off many of the complications for years due to your physical regimen of hiking, biking, dancing, and more.

You'll look great in whatever wedding dress you choose, much better than I would. With that in mind, you may not borrow my ensemble. I do not wish to be shown up by my little sister.

Ricky,

You make me laugh and you encourage me. Thanks for both.

Little Ru,

The trouble with the word "encourage" is that no matter what I say, you're the courageous one. I merely watch safely from the bleachers, admire and cheer.

Ricky,

You cannot imagine how much that means to me. I have my equilibrium back today, feels much better.

Baby sister Ru,

That's great news! Let's stay in touch, address a dress, and get it off of your list.

Your big brother,
Rick

BOB
(1-22-2008)

Dear little sisters, Ru and Bun,

I'm hoping that you'll get a kick out of this recent incident:

My new well-meaning, millennial neighbor, Bob, asked, "Isn't there someone younger who could clear your driveway after that snowstorm? We got at least eleven inches overnight. It's got to be tough on your heart and your back."

I replied from the end of my driveway while standing in the four-foot drift left behind by the snowplow, "When my two, twenty-something girlfriends and I woke up this morning, after some 'cuddling,' we noticed the new snowfall."

The twins agreed, "Hef, we'll do almost anything for you, but there are three things that we'll never do."

I asked, "Based on our get-togethers these past few months, I'm curious as to what they may be."

Isabella replied, "Shoveling snow."

Angelica, the talkative twin, added, "That's right. And, we won't mud wrestle while wearing the bikinis that Signore Armani designed especially for us."

I commented, "Angelica, I wouldn't ask for you two to do such a thing."

She replied, "Oh, I'm glad, Hef. Just so you know, we'll never call you 'Rick' when 'Hef' seems so natural."

Later, after I finished our driveway, Bob was honored to have my assistance.

#####

RU AND A BELLY DANCER
(12-09-2009)

Ricky,

Two owls in the woods behind our condo have been serenading Terry and me at night. One has deep staccato hoots of five beats (long, short, short, short, long) and the other has higher-pitched, short hoots of two beats. We figure they're love birds singing to each other, and we're the fortunate ones who hear and marvel at it.

###

Little Ru,

Certainly the male owl is showing much interest with its five hoots. He's lucky. In my experience, the female doesn't give two hoots.

###

Ru, baby sister,

These are a few of the words and their meanings that come to mind whenever I think of Ru.

- **Ru**bella: A disease that could be transmitted by Ru's punishing punches, and a belly dancer.

- **Ru**bicund: The facial color of a maddened baby sister.

- **Ru**bric: The end product of Ru's seven-day bout with constipation, and Ru's fist when she's Rubicund.

- **Ru**bic: A cube named for Ru. She's always been more than square.

- **Ru**de: Any baby sister.

- **Ru**dimentary: Ru's intellectual capacity after one glass of wine.

- **Ru**minate: A class of animals named for Ru's feet and chewing style.

- **Ru**um: What shoes need once Ru installs her feet.

- **Ru**e: A word I use after Ru removes her foot apparel.

- **Ru**se: A mean baby-sister trick.

- **Ru**in: My dates when I tell stories about my childhood with Ru.

- **Ru**mania: Baby sister laughing at the dumbest jokes ever, ever.

- **Ru**pee: The results of Rumania.

- **Ru**nestone: An artifact with ancient writings upon which Ru modeled her cursive.

- **Ru**bel: What Ru did as a teenager, and a belly dancer.

- **Ru**bber: Forget that I listed it.

- **Ru**le: What Ru does by threatening, "I'm going to tell."

- **Ru**ler: A tool Ru uses to smack me.

- **Ru**n: What I do when Ru has a ruler.

- **Ru**bs: What Ru has always done to her brother, the wrong way.

- **Ru**mp: Something Ru and I don't possess.

- **Ru**ng: What you did to my neck … often.

- **Ru**bens: Never mind. The visuals, oh save me, the visuals.

- **Ru**thenium: Like Ru, a rare, valuable element, which doesn't tarnish unless it comes in contact with the Beach Boys.

- **Rw**anda: A country that sounds like combining Ru and her given name, Rhonda.

- **Ru**thless: Yes she is, and what happened when I told my former girlfriend Ruth stories about my childhood with Ru.

- **Ru**mble: What Ru and I did often as kids, and the sound that Ru's stomach makes after she's eaten too much mint dessert.

- **Ru**mor: Ru always wants more, in particular, mint dessert.

- **Ru**mer: Daughter of Bruce Willis and Demi Moore named after my baby sister.

- **Ru**by: The gem that IS my baby sister, most often found in the navel of a belly dancer.

Ok, that's enough, unless **Ru**mor.
Your big brother,
Ricky

#####

GENDER
(12-23-2009)

Little sisters,

According to my yardstick, the skies gifted us with two inches of beautifully falling, light, fluffy snow late yesterday afternoon. Overnight, the same benefactor barfed up fourteen inches of heavy, detestable slop.

Minutes after I came inside from shoveling the driveway, a snowplow came through and donated a three-foot pile of that puke onto the rear end of our driveway. As an added bonus, it broke off the mailbox post that Cora had painted yellow late last fall so that the snowplow drivers couldn't miss it.

Removing that mess can wait until I thaw out, but I've got to get that gender-specific job taken care of before nightfall. Otherwise, the below-zero temperatures will freeze the discolored barf into a giant banana Popsicle, accented by our mailbox beam.

It's 7 p.m., well after dark, below zero, and I haven't started shoveling yet. There may be a bright spot to my procrastination. I'm considering a sauna, followed by a nearly naked snow-bath. Unfortunately, my head, hands and feet are susceptible to freezing and cracking. So, I'll wear a fur hat with a chin strap, waterproof gloves, and hunting boots. I'm going for it!

That was an extraordinary experience. None of my body parts fractured in the cold, but my gender is not readily apparent.

#####

Banter Battles

"So, Wifey, you're going to save my ashes in an ice cream bucket instead of an urn?"

"I've changed my mind, Hubber,"

"Oh, I've come up in the world?"

"No, you've got no butt, so I should be able to fit them in a cottage cheese container."

I bragged, "I'm a badass."

Cora replied, "You have to own one for it to be bad."

Quips and Quotes

Two weeks after we got married, November 20, 1971, Cora gave birth to Women's Lib. Forty-nine years later, that kid is still libbing at home!

At the dinner table, I complained, "I'm hunting for the appropriate words to finish this book. It's haunting me."

Noah commented, "THE END."

###

ACKNOWLEDGEMENTS

Ru and Bun, the best sisters a guy could ever have...mostly.

Ru captioned this picture, "My favorite brother Rick and his wife Cora walking through life together."

Cora commented, "There's light at the end of the tunnel. You walk towards it. I'll wait here."

ABOUT THE AUTHOR

C ora the Dish and Rick are retired and live in Sun Prairie, Wisconsin not far from their three sons and daughters-in-law, and seven grandchildren.

Cora the Dish, Rick, and granddaughter Annabelle.